Anonymous

Form of Prayer, and a New Collection of Psalms

For the use of a congregation of Protestant Dissenters in Liverpool

Anonymous

Form of Prayer, and a New Collection of Psalms
For the use of a congregation of Protestant Dissenters in Liverpool

ISBN/EAN: 9783337042462

Printed in Europe, USA, Canada, Australia, Japan

Cover: Foto ©Lupo / pixelio.de

More available books at **www.hansebooks.com**

FORM of PRAYER,

AND

A New Collection of PSALMS,

FOR THE USE OF

A CONGREGATION

OF

PROTESTANT DISSENTERS

IN

LIVERPOOL.

PRINTED FOR THE SOCIETY;

AND SOLD BY

CHR. HENDERSON, under the ROYAL EXCHANGE, LONDON;

AND BY

JOHN SIBBALD, Bookseller, in LIVERPOOL.

M DCC LXIII.

Advertisement.

THESE Compositions are not the hasty production of any one person, but the joint labour of several, improved by the judicious remarks of many. The Society, for whose use they were drawn up, have now made them public; and hope they will receive many farther improvements, from the candid examination of those who have not yet perused them.

Until suitable offices are composed for BAPTISM, and the LORD'S SUPPER, these rites will be administered as usual among PROTESTANT DISSENTERS.

MORNING SERVICE.

¶ *The* Morning Service *is to be introduced by the following* Addreſs, *from the Miniſter to the People, the congregation riſing up.*

Miniſter.

'O BE joyful in the LORD all
' ye people: ſerve the LORD
' with gladneſs; and enter into
' his courts with praiſe.
   ' Know ye that the LORD he is
' GOD; it is he who hath made us,
' and not we ourſelves; we are his
' people, and the ſheep of his paſture.
   ' Let us come into his preſence with
' thankſgiving: let us give unto the
' LORD the glory due unto his name.
   ' For the LORD is GOOD; his MERCY
' is everlaſting; and his TRUTH endureth
' to all generations.'

B   *People.*

People.
Unto the LORD *our* GOD *will we lift up our souls, and magnify his name together.*

¶ *The* Introductory Prayer; *to be read by the Minister alone.*

O HOLY, holy, LORD GOD almighty, before whom all creatures bow; may we celebrate thy perfections, and speak of thy wonderful works, with attention and reverence; give thanks unto thee, and sing thy praises, with joy and gladness; humble ourselves before thee with sincere, and contrite hearts; and pray unto thee under a just sense of our dependence upon thy providence; and with fervent charity to all men: and may these our devotions, which we offer up in the name, and as the disciples of JESUS CHRIST, be acceptable to thee, O GOD, our strength and our redeemer. *Amen.*

This

MORNING SERVICE.

¶ *This HYMN for celebrating the* Divine Perfections; *or the following, for celebrating the* Divine Works, *is to be recited by the Minister and People alternately, all standing.*

Minister.

WE praise thee, O GOD; we worship thee, the most glorious and excellent being; the creator and governor of all things, visible and invisible.

We praise and worship the most high GOD; *who is*

People.

O LORD GOD, thou art greatly to be praised; and to be had in reverence by all who draw nigh unto thee.

Minister.

We acknowledge thee, the one, living, and true GOD: GOD in heaven above, and earth beneath, and throughout all worlds: there is none besides thee.

One,

People.

MORNING SERVICE.

People.
Unto us there is but one GOD; to whom be glory for ever.

Minister.

Eternal, Thou alone art from everlasting, without beginning of days, or end of years; thou livest, and reignest for ever and ever.

People.
We magnify thee, the high and lofty One, who inhabitest eternity.

Minister.

Invisible, Thou art a spiritual and incorruptible being; who dwellest in light inaccessible, and full of glory; whom no mortal eye hath seen, or can see.

People.
We would worship thee, who art a spirit, in spirit and in truth.

Minister.

Omnipresent, Infinite art thou, O GOD: thou dwellest not in temples made with hands; the universe is thy temple; thou art present at all times in every part of thy dominion.

Peo-

MORNING SERVICE.

People.

In thee we live, and move, and have our being.

Miniſter.

Thine is the greatneſs, and the power, and the glory, and the majeſty: all things in heaven and in earth are thine: thine is the kingdom, and thou art to be worſhiped as LORD over all. <small>Omnipotent,</small>

People.

Thou art great, and greatly to be feared; thy greatneſs is unſearchable.

Miniſter.

Thou art perfect in wiſdom, wonderful in council, and excellent in all thy works. <small>Omniſcient,</small>

People.

To the only wiſe GOD, be honour and glory for ever.

Miniſter.

Holy art thou, O GOD; thou art of purer eyes than to behold iniquity; thy countenance regardeth the upright. <small>Holy,</small>

Peo-

People.

We reverence thy name; for thou art holy.

Minister.

Just, Thy righteousness is like the great mountains; thy truth reacheth to the heavens: justice and judgment are the everlasting foundations of thy throne.

People.

Just and true are all thy ways, O thou king of saints.

Minister.

and Good; Thou art good, thou doest good continually; the earth is full of thy goodness; and all thy works bear testimony to thy rich and overflowing bounty: every good, and every perfect gift is from above, and cometh down from thee the FATHER OF ALL.

People.

O LORD, thy goodness is above all praise; universal as thy works, and endless as eternity.

Mini-

Minister.

All glory and honour; blessing and praise; might, majesty and dominion be unto GOD for ever. *Amen.*

to whom be Glory for ever.

¶ *Instead of the foregoing, may be used, at the choice of the Minister, the following* HYMN, *for celebrating the* DIVINE WORKS.

Minister.

O GOD the Creator and governor of all things; we praise thee, we worship thee, the most excellent and glorious being, infinite and unchangeable in power, wisdom, and goodness.

General Act of Praise to GOD

People.

Power, wisdom, and goodness, are thine, O LORD.

Minister.

We praise thee, O GOD, we magnify thee, for making known unto us these thy perfections; and

for Knowledge of him by his Works.

and that by thy works which we behold, thou art leading us to the contemplation and love of thee, the fountain of life, and the author of all good.

People.

With our whole hearts will we praise thee; and speak of thy marvellous works.

Minister.

<small>General View of the Works of GOD.</small> With admiration and joy do we behold the beauty, order, and magnificence of thy creation: thereby are we led to acknowledge thine eternal being and providence; and to worship thee, the author and conductor of all things.

People.

All thy works praise thee, and we thy people bless thee.

Minister.

<small>The heavenly Bodies,</small> In wisdom hast thou stretched out the firmament, and the heavens are the work of thy hands; the sun, moon, and stars thou hast

hast ordained to fulfil thy pleasure: these declare thine almighty power, and universal goodness.

People.

The heavens, and all the hosts of heaven worship thee.

Minister.

The air which we breathe is thy wise provision; thou coverest the heavens with clouds; thou preparest the rain, and the dew; thou causest thy winds to blow; thou sendest forth thy commandment; all things are obedient to the voice of thy word. *Air.*

People.

These are thy wonderful works; thy name be praised for ever.

Minister.

Of old hast thou laid the foundations of the earth: thou hast cloathed it with grass; furnished it with herbs; adorned it with flowers; and enriched it with every thing necessary for the support and happiness of thy creatures. Peo- *Earth.*

People.

The earth is thine, O LORD, *thou haſt filled it with the riches of thy goodneſs.*

Miniſter.

Seaſons, The conſtant ſucceſſion of day and night; and the grateful return of ſummer and winter, ſeedtime and harveſt, are the gracious appointments of thy providence.

People.

The day is thine; the night alſo is thine; thy goodneſs endureth for ever.

Miniſter.

Animal World, The birds of the air, the fiſhes of the ſea, and the cattle upon a thouſand hills are thine; thou ſendeſt forth thy ſpirit, they are created; thou reneweſt the face of the Earth.

People.

Thou openeſt thy hand; they are filled with good.

Mini-

Minifter.

Thou art the Creator, and Father of mankind; thou haft made us in thine own image, to contemplate thy works, and fhew forth thy praife. *Mankind.*

People.

We are thine offspring; we will praife and exalt thee for ever.

Minifter.

Great and marvellous are all thy works, O LORD GOD almighty! thou haft made heaven, and the heaven of heavens, with all their hofts; the earth, and all the things that are therein; the fea, and all that is in it; and thou preferveft them continually.

People.

O LORD, how manifold are thy works!---In wifdom haft thou made them all.

¶ *Here*

MORNING SERVICE.

¶ *Here the* First Lesson *is to be read out of the* Holy Scriptures; *after which the* Service *is to proceed with the following* Thanksgivings; *the congregation rising up.*

Minister.

" LET us now offer up unto GOD
" our sincere and humble thanksgivings,
" for his great goodness to us, and to
" all mankind.
" O give thanks unto the LORD
" ye his people, give thanks at the
" remembrance of his goodness.
" Let us meditate upon his mercies
" with delight; and let the words of
" our mouths, and the actions of our
" lives, shew forth his praise."

People.

Bless the LORD, O our souls, and forget not all his benefits.

Minister.

General Act of Thanksgiving

WE thank thee, O Father, LORD of heaven and earth, for the innumerable mercies

MORNING SERVICE.

cies thou haft beftowed upon us. We acknowledge, with all gratitude and joy, the gift of life: thine almighty voice hath called us into being; and thy hand hath placed us in this part of thy glorious works. *for Creation,*

We thank thee for the wife and ufeful frame of our bodies; and for the nobler powers of our minds; by which we are enabled to contemplate the beauty of thy works, and the wonderful order of thy providence; and to attain to the knowledge, and love of thee, the Creator of the world, and the Author of all good. *Powers of Body and Mind,*

We thank thee that thou haft implanted in us a fenfe of good and evil; and the amiable affections of benevolence and compaffion; hereby leading us to the admiration and love of goodnefs; and to the enjoyment of that happinefs, which arifes from the practice of virtue, and true religion. " O

MORNING SERVICE.

"O that men would praise the LORD for his goodness; and for his wonderful works to the children of men."

People.

We praise the LORD for his goodness; and for his wonderful works to the children of men.

Minister.

Preservative and Blessings of Life.

We thank thee, O ever bountiful and most gracious GOD, for the continual preservation of our lives: in thy hand is the life of every living creature, and the breath of all mankind: our food and raiment are the daily gifts of thy bounty: thou givest us healthful and fruitful seasons, and fillest our hearts with joy and gladness: the blessings of friendship, liberty, and equal government, are thy wise and benevolent appointment.

"O that men would praise the LORD for his goodness; and for his wonderful works to the children of men."

MORNING SERVICE.

People.

We praise the LORD for his goodness; and for his wonderful works to the children of men.

Minister.

We bless thee, O heavenly Father, that thy goodness to mankind is not confined to this present world; but that thou hast awakened in us the pleasing hope of immortality; and by the various means of thy providence and grace, art training us up for a heavenly and everlasting life. *Hope of Immortality,*

We thank thee for the instructions and examples of wise and good men in every age; and for every opportunity of attaining that measure of knowledge and virtue which is necessary to our happiness. *Means of Improvement,*

But above all we praise and magnify thee, for the rich display of thy goodness, in the manifestation of thy Son CHRIST JESUS; whom thou hast raised *Salvation by JESUS CHRIST.*

up

up to bleſs mankind; to turn them from darkneſs to light; and from the power of ſin, to the worſhip and obedience of thee, the true GOD.

We acknowledge with the higheſt gratitude, the perfect doctrine of our bleſſed Saviour; that by him thou haſt given us thy heavenly truth; to enlighten our minds, to ſanctify our hearts, and guide our feet in the way of peace; and that in his life thou haſt ſet before us an example of the moſt exalted goodneſs, to animate our endeavours, and to encourage us to preſs forward continually.

We thank thee for the promiſes of thy mercy and forgiveneſs, upon repentance, and newneſs of life; for the aſſurance of thy gracious influence to help our infirmities; and for the bleſſed hope of immortality, confirmed to us in the Goſpel.

We rejoice in the exceeding riches of thy grace; that thou haſt exalted thy Son JESUS to be a Prince, and a Saviour; and that through thy wiſe and merciful

merciful appointment, he is the Author of eternal salvation to all those who obey him.

"O that men would praise the LORD
"for his goodness; and for his wonderful
"works to the children of men."

People.

Blessed be the GOD *and Father of our* LORD JESUS CHRIST, *for his goodness; and for his wonderful works to the children of men.*

¶ *Here a* Psalm of Praise, *or* Thanksgiving *is to be sung*; *and after that the* Second Lesson *read, out of the* NEW TESTAMENT.

¶ *Then the* Service *must proceed with the following* Address, *the congregation rising up.*

Minister.

"IF we say we have no sin, we de-
"ceive ourselves, and the truth is not
"in us.

"If

"If we confefs and forfake our fins, GOD is faithful and juft to forgive us, and to cleanfe us from all unrighteoufnefs.

"Let us therefore, my chriftian brethren, with humble and contrite hearts confefs our fins at the throne of the heavenly grace."

¶ *The* General Confession; *to be read by the Minifter alone, the whole Congregation kneeling.*

ALMIGHTY GOD, Father of our LORD JESUS CHRIST, Maker of all things, and Judge of all men: we acknowledge and lament before thee, the manifold errors and follies of our lives: we have not duly hearkened to the voice of thy word: we have followed too much the devices and defires of our own hearts: we have been too unmindful of thy goodnefs; and ungrateful to thee, our continual benefactor: we have not always done unto others as we would that they fhould do unto us: we have departed

MORNING SERVICE.

departed from the ways of thy commandments; and exposed ourselves to thy righteous displeasure: our only hope is in thy mercy, which endureth for ever. We bow ourselves before the throne of thy grace, imploring thy pardon: O GOD have mercy upon the work of thy hands: hear our supplications, we beseech thee: forgive and accept thy people; according to thy promises by CHRIST JESUS, our LORD; and may we hereafter live a godly, righteous, and sober life, to the glory of thy holy name. *Amen.*

¶ *Then the following* Prayers *are to be read, the congregation still kneeling, and saying* Amen, *at the conclusion of each* Prayer.

A Prayer for Repentance and Pardon.

O Gracious GOD, our heavenly Father, who desirest not the death of a sinner, but rather that he may turn from his wickedness and live; and hast encouraged us to hope for thy mercy upon repentance, and amendment of life; we desire, with our whole hearts, to return to the obedience of thy commandments: may we from henceforth forsake every evil way; correct whatever is wrong in our temper and conduct; and delight in the practice of every thing good and virtuous; that we may obtain from thee, the GOD of all mercy, the forgiveness of our sins; and an inheritance among those who are sanctified. *Amen.*

For religious Wisdom.

O FATHER of lights, and fountain of knowledge, open the eyes of our minds, and enlighten us with true wisdom: may we have pure and worthy apprehensions of thy nature and providence: lead us to a right understanding of that religion which is acceptable to thee, and recommended to us in the Gospel of thy Son: may we evermore discern, approve, and practice, the things which are excellent; and by a life devoted

voted to thy service, be prepared for the glorious and everlasting kingdom of our Lord and Saviour JESUS CHRIST. *Amen.*

For good Dispositions.

EVER blessed and most holy GOD, who searchest the hearts of men; and before all things regardest the virtuous and upright mind; we beseech thee that our hearts may be endued with every good and pious disposition: and that all the great truths of religion may have a powerful and lasting influence, in correcting the vices of our minds, and amending the disorders of our lives; that by purity and righteousness, we may approve ourselves to thee, the judge of all the earth. *Amen.*

Piety to GOD.

WE desire at all times, to retain a most devout sense, and holy admiration, of thine excellent nature; to reverence thine authority; to look up unto

unto thee with satisfaction and joy, as the giver of all good; to love thee with all our hearts; to delight in thy service; to be thankful for thine innumerable, and undeserved mercies; to confide in thine all-gracious providence; and to yield an unreserved, and grateful obedience, to all thy holy commandments. *Amen.*

Charity to Mankind.

AS children of the GOD of all love and mercy; as members of the society of mankind; and the common disciples of JESUS, we desire to put on bowels of mercy, kindness, compassion, humbleness of mind, meekness, long-suffering; forbearing one another, forgiving one another. We would do unto all men, as we desire they should do unto us; and in the constant exercise of justice and honesty, humanity and mercy, fulfil the gracious purposes of thy providence, and live in peace and charity with all men. *Amen.*

Self-

Self-government.

UNDER a deep sense of our obligations, as thine offspring, and the sacred duties of our profession, as the disciples of JESUS, who hath called us to glory and virtue, and the joyful hope of immortality, we earnestly desire to maintain a constant government over ourselves; to be sober, chaste, and temperate in all things; and to direct our views to a future state, in joyful expectation of thy mercy unto eternal life. *Amen.*

For Sincerity.

O Ever present, most holy, and righteous God! before whom all things are open; may our hearts be upright in thy sight: in whatever station thou art pleased to appoint our lot; and wherever we are, in public, or in private, may it be our uniform and steady purpose, to discharge our duty with fidelity: may we never remove our integrity from us: and in that solemn day when thou

thou supreme over all, shalt judge the world by JESUS CHRIST, may we be able to appear with humble confidence and joy; and be admitted into his glorious and everlasting kingdom. *Amen.*

Submission to the Divine Providence.

O LORD GOD, whose never-failing providence ordereth all things both in heaven and in earth, and who art the Author of every good and perfect gift; we submit ourselves to the disposal of that wisdom which cannot err, and to the care of that goodness which is unchangeable and everlasting: lead us whither thou pleasest; place us in what circumstances thou shalt judge proper: we would do thy whole will with fidelity and pleasure; we would bear thy whole will with submission and patience: defend us, O gracious Father, from every real evil; confer upon us every needful good; may all events conspire to the improvement and establishment of our virtue; and may we be conducted by thine

thine unerring hand, through all the changes of this mortal life, and finally admitted to the everlasting habitations of the just, which thou haft promised to thy faithful servants by JESUS CHRIST, our LORD. *Amen.*

¶ *Instead of the following* Prayers, *the* GENERAL INTERCESSION *may be read, at the choice of the Minister.*

A Prayer for all Mankind.

ALMIGHTY, and everlasting GOD, who haft taught us to offer up prayers, supplications, and intercessions for all men, we beseech thee to extend thy mercy and favour to all mankind: may all the families and kingdoms of the earth be brought to the knowledge, and pure worship of thee, the only true GOD: enlarge the kingdom of our LORD JESUS CHRIST, that kingdom of truth and righteousness, which shall never be destroyed: put an end to all idolatry, superstition, and false religion:

may pure, and uncorrupted Christianity prevail: may all who profess the faith of CHRIST, be shining examples of goodness: may the spirit of persecution for ever cease; and may truth and righteousness, peace and charity, every where abound. *Amen.*

For our Country.

O LORD GOD, high and mighty, who dost from thy throne behold all the dwellers upon earth; look down with favour and mercy upon the kingdoms of GREAT BRITAIN and IRELAND, and all our colonies and provinces: may a speedy and effectual stop be put to the progress of immorality and profaneness: may public virtue prevail; and on that lasting foundation, may the public happiness be established: may our liberties be preserved inviolate, and handed down to the latest posterity. Bless us with healthful times, and fruitful seasons: crown the year with thy goodness: dispose us all to a grateful and temperate enjoy-

enjoyment of the bounties of thy providence; and may we shew forth thy praise, not only with our lips, but in our lives; by giving up ourselves to thy service, and walking before thee, in holiness and righteousness, all our days. *Amen.*

For the King.

ALMIGHTY GOD, the king of kings, and lord of lords, we humbly beseech thee to send down the choicest of thy blessings upon thy servant GEORGE our king: in wisdom and righteousness, in justice and clemency, may he rule thy people: may all his endeavours to promote the virtue and happiness, and to perpetuate the freedom of his subjects, be crowned with success: may the years of his government be many, prosperous, and happy: may we evermore have reason to rejoice in him, as the minister of thy providence to us for good; and may he at length be rewarded in thy heavenly and everlasting kingdom. *Amen.*

MORNING SERVICE.

For the Queen and Royal Family.

O GOD the fountain of all goodness, we beseech thee to visit, with thine especial favour, our gracious Queen CHARLOTTE; the Prince of WALES; the Princess Dowager of WALES; and all the Royal Family: may they cultivate all those amiable and princely virtues, which will render them the ornaments of their high stations, and extensive blessings to mankind: grant them happiness in this world, and in that which is to come, life everlasting. *Amen.*

For the Nobility and Magistrates.

MAY it please thee, O GOD, the fountain of all power, to bless the king's counsellors, the nobility, judges, and the whole body of the magistracy of this land: may they do the duties of their stations with understanding and wisdom, with integrity and honour; and under them may we, and all thy people, lead peaceable and quiet lives, in all
godli-

godlineſs and honeſty; keeping the unity of the ſpirit, in the bond of peace, and righteouſneſs of life. *Amen.*

For the Parliament.

[*To be read only when ſitting.*]

O GOD of infinite wiſdom, preſide we intreat thee, in the great council of the nation, at this time in parliament aſſembled; direct and proſper all their conſultations, to the advancement of thy glory; the good of thy church; the ſafety, honour, and welfare of our ſovereign, and his kingdoms: and may all things be ſo ordered by their endeavours, that peace and liberty, truth and juſtice, religion and virtue, may be eſtabliſhed amongſt us, to all generations. *Amen.*

For the Miniſters of Religion.

O GOD, the Father of lights, and fountain of all good, endue the miniſters of thy true religion, of every denomi-

denomination, and in every part of the Christian world, with the spirit and temper of CHRIST JESUS: may they diligently pursue the good work of instructing the ignorant, and reforming the vicious; and in all the duties of their office may they conduct themselves, not as having dominion over the faith of Christians, but as examples to their flocks; and by the excellency of their doctrines, and the holiness of their lives, may they save themselves, and those who hear them. *Amen.*

For those who are in Affliction.

MOST merciful, and gracious GOD, the GOD of all consolation and good hope, we humbly recommend to thy fatherly goodness, all those who are any-ways afflicted, or distressed, in mind, body, or estate: [*those especially for whom our prayers are desired*] be thou, in thy great mercy, a father to the fatherless; and the defender of the widow; provide for the poor; give health to the sick;

MORNING SERVICE.

sick; and ease to those who are in pain; deliver those who are oppressed; and comfort those who mourn: support thy faithful servants who are in bonds, or in any manner persecuted for righteousness sake; give them fortitude in the day of trial, and, in due time, a happy deliverance out of all their afflictions. And from the various calamities we meet with in human life, either in ourselves or others, may we learn to pity the distressed; to mourn with those who mourn; to be patient under all the appointments of thy providence; and be excited to the pursuit of that happiness, which ariseth from the practice of virtue and religion, and the glorious hope of immortality: and this we ask in the name, and as the disciples of JESUS CHRIST, our Lord and Saviour. *Amen.*

Concluding Prayer.

O LORD, our heavenly Father, almighty and everlasting GOD, who hast safely brought us to the return of this

this day; and haſt permitted us to make our united ſupplications unto thee; defend us through the ſame, by thy grace and power. Accept the praiſes, and hear the prayers we have offered up to thy divine majeſty: and fulfil, O LORD, the deſires and petitions of thy ſervants, as may be moſt expedient for them; granting us in this world, knowledge of thy truth, and in the world to come, life everlaſting. *Amen.*

OUR Father, who art in heaven; hallowed be thy name: thy kingdom come: thy will be done on earth as it is in heaven: give us this day our daily bread; and forgive us our treſpaſſes, as we forgive thoſe who treſpaſs againſt us; and lead us not into temptation; but deliver us from evil: for thine is the kingdom, and the power, and the glory, for ever and ever. *Amen.*

¶ *Here a* Pſalm *muſt be ſung, while the Miniſter is preparing for the pulpit.*

¶ *The*

¶ *The* Benediction *is to be pronounced by the Minister, at the conclusion of the whole Service.*

¶ *Instead of the foregoing* Prayers, *the following* GENERAL INTERCESSION *may be used, at the choice of the Minister.*

THE

General Intercession.

O GOD, the Creator of heaven and earth, the common Father of all mankind; we thy servants do beseech thee to hear us, not only in our prayers for ourselves, but in our intercessions for all our brethren and fellow creatures: make thy ways known upon earth, and thy saving health unto all nations; that all mankind may be united in the pure and holy worship of thee, the true and living GOD, as the disciples of JESUS CHRIST, whom thou hast sent. *Amen.*

F   Send

Send down thy heavenly blessing upon every part of the Christian world: put an end to all persecution, and usurpation over the judgments and consciences of mankind; lead all professing Christians to the right understanding and practice of our holy religion; unite their minds in charity and godly love; and may their light so shine before men, that others seeing their good works, may glorify thee, our Father, who art in heaven. *Amen.*

In thine own due time, put an end to all the disorders and calamities introduced into this world, by the pride, ambition, and tyranny of wicked men; and give unto all mankind unity, peace, and concord. *Amen.*

Preserve the peace, liberty, and happiness of our native country; defend us from the designs of our enemies, and from all great and wasting calamities; and confirm, and continue to us, that wise and equal government, under which,

in

MORNING SERVICE.   35

in thy great mercy, thou haft placed us. *Amen.*

Keep and ftrengthen in the true worfhipping of thee, in righteoufnefs and holinefs of life, thy fervant GEORGE, our moft gracious king: eftablifh his heart in thy faith, fear, and love: may he evermore confide in thee, and feek thy honour and glory; and be thou his defender and keeper, giving him the victory over all our enemies. *Amen.*

Blefs and preferve our gracious Queen CHARLOTTE; the Prince of WALES; the Princefs Dowager of WALES; and all the Royal Family. *Amen.*

May the lords of the council, and all the nobility, be eminent for wifdom, piety, and virtue. *Amen.*

[Prefide in the high court of parliament, at this time affembled; and over-rule all their debates and confultations, for the public good. *Amen.*] *To be read only when the Parliament is fitting.*

Blefs

Blefs the judges, and all the magiſtrates of theſe lands: may they execute juſtice; maintain peace; be a terror to evil-doers; and a protection to thoſe who do well. *Amen.*

Blefs the miniſters of the Chriſtian religion, with true knowledge, and underſtanding of thy word: may they be faithful in the diſcharge of their important duty; that by the power of truth, and the influence of a good example, they may turn many to righteouſnefs. *Amen.*

Blefs our univerſities, and all ſchools and ſeminaries of learning: may they promote the true principles of religion, virtue, and liberty; and may all uſeful knowledge more generally prevail. *Amen.*

Blefs all thy people: difpoſe their hearts truly to fear and love thee; to receive thy word with pure affection; to do the duties of their ſeveral ſtations with fidelity; to bring forth the fruits of the ſpirit;

MORNING SERVICE.

ſpirit; and diligently to live after thy commandments. *Amen.*

Bring into the way of truth all ſuch as have erred, and are deceived; ſtrengthen ſuch as do ſtand; raiſe up thoſe who fall; comfort thoſe who mourn; bind up the broken-hearted; aſſiſt all who are in neceſſity or trouble; and have compaſſion upon all who are afflicted. *Amen.*

Preſerve all thoſe who are travelling by land or by water; all women labouring with child; all ſick perſons, and young children: ſupport the aged; provide for the fatherleſs, and widows, and all who are deſolate and oppreſſed; and ſhew thy mercy to all priſoners and captives; eſpecially to ſuch as are ſuffering for righteouſneſs ſake. *Amen.*

Bleſs our friends; reward our benefactors; forgive our enemies, perſecutors, and ſlanderers; and turn their hearts.

People,

People.

May it pleaſe thee, O GOD, *to have mercy upon all men.*

Miniſter.

May the GOD, and Father of our LORD JESUS CHRIST, the Father of mercies, the GOD of all conſolations, hear our prayers.

People.

Gracioufly hear us, O GOD, *our heavenly Father.*

A concluding Prayer.

Miniſter.

ALMIGHTY and moſt merciful GOD, who haſt permitted us at this time, with one accord to make our common ſupplications unto thee; fulfil the deſires and petitions of thy ſervants, as may be moſt expedient for them; granting us in this world knowledge of thy truth; and in the world to come life everlaſting. Amen.

¶ *Here a* Pſalm *muſt be ſung, while the Miniſter is preparing for the pulpit.*

EVENING

EVENING SERVICE.

¶ *This* Service *muſt be introduced by the following* Addreſs, *from the Miniſter to the People, the congregation riſing up.*

Miniſter.

"HEAR all ye people, give ear all
" ye inhabitants of the world;
" for the LORD GOD omnipotent
" reigneth. Let the heaven and the
" earth praiſe him; the ſeas, and every
" thing that moveth therein. Sing unto
" the LORD, and give thanks at the
" remembrance of his goodneſs. Truſt
" in him at all times, ye people; pour
" out your hearts before him; for
" GOD is our refuge. He knoweth
" our thoughts, and will render to every
" man according to his works. Offer
" therefore unto him the ſacrifices of
" righteouſneſs; for in his preſence is
" fulneſs

EVENING SERVICE.

"fulness of joy, and at his right hand
"are pleasures for evermore."

People.

The LORD *reigneth;* let the earth rejoice.

¶ *The* Introductory Prayer; *to be read by the Minister alone.*

O EVER blessed, and most glorious LORD our GOD, the object of supreme veneration, on whom all the families of the earth continually depend: we would present ourselves before thee with reverence and humility: we would offer up unto thee our sacrifices of praise and thanksgiving, with joy and gratitude. By celebrating thy perfections, may we be excited to an ardent love and imitation of thee, our Father in heaven: and may the remembrance of thy great goodness to us, and to all mankind, incline us to love and serve one another as brethren. May we confess our sins with unfeigned sorrow, and steady purposes of amendment: may we we pray unto thee, as the bountiful dispenser of every good thing: may our intercessions be accompanied with charity to all men: may we serve thee with freedom and delight; and keep a watchful guard over ourselves, at all times; more especially whilst we are employed in the awful and important duties of thy house: may no vain thoughts distract our minds; no unworthy object withdraw our affections; but may our whole hearts be engaged in thy worship; and the influence of these our religious services be abundantly shewn forth in the actions of our lives. All which we pray for in the name, and as the disciples of JESUS CHRIST, our LORD. *Amen.*

¶ *Then the following* HYMN, *for celebrating the* Divine Perfections, *is to be recited by the Minister and People alternately, all standing.*

Minister.

We praise the true, and living GOD,

WE praise thee, O GOD, we worship thee, the one, true, and living GOD; who art infinite, and unchangeable, in all thy perfections.

People.

Blessed art thou, O LORD GOD, and worthy to be praised for ever.

Minister.

the Creator, and Preserver; who is

Thou, O GOD, art king of kings, lord of lords, the great and only potentate, the Creator and Preserver of all things: thou didst speak, and the world was made; thy providence supports the works of thy hands; and the happiness of thy creatures, is the end of all.

People.

EVENING SERVICE.

People.
Thou art God over all, blessed for evermore.

Minister.
Before the mountains were brought forth, or ever thou hadst formed the earth, and the world; from everlasting to everlasting, thou art GOD. *Eternal,*

People.
Thou livest, and reignest for ever.

Minister.
Thou art the LORD, and changest not: of old hast thou laid the foundations of the earth; and the heavens are the work of thy hands: these shall perish, but thou shalt endure; thy counsel standeth fast; and thy thoughts unto all generations. *Immutable,*

People.
Thou art the same yesterday, to-day, and for ever.

EVENING SERVICE.

Minister.

Invisible, We adore and worship thee, a pure and spiritual being, whom no man hath seen, or can see: thou passest by us on every side, but we behold thee not: thou continually workest wonders on the right hand, and on the left; but we do not perceive thee.

People.

Thou art a spirit; and they who worship thee, must worship in spirit, and in truth.

Minister.

Omnipresent, Whither can we flee from thy presence! heaven is thy throne; the earth thy footstool; and the universe thy habitation.

People.

All things are full of thee.

Minister.

Omnipotent, Who can withstand thy power! the mountains shake from their foundations; the rocks melt like wax; and the earth trembleth at thy presence: thou doest whatever

ever thou pleaseſt in the armies of heaven, and among the inhabitants of the world.

People.

With the LORD our GOD is everlaſting ſtrength.

Miniſter.

Thou haſt founded the earth by thy wiſdom; and ſtretched out the heavens by thine underſtanding: by thy knowledge the depths are broken up, and the clouds drop down the dew: thou art mighty in wiſdom, wonderful in counſel, and excellent in all thy works. *Wiſe.*

People.

O LORD, how manifold are thy works! in wiſdom haſt thou made them all.

Miniſter.

Thou art the righteous LORD, who exerciſeſt judgment in the earth: thy righteouſneſs is like the great mountains; thy faithfulneſs reacheth above the clouds; eternal truth is thy law. *Juſt.*

People.

Upright art thou, O LORD; all thy works are juſt and true.

Miniſter.

Holy, O LORD GOD, holy and reverend is thy name: thou art of purer eyes than to behold iniquity: ſinners cannot ſtand before thee; but the upright in heart are always in the light of thy countenance.

People.

We reverence thee, O GOD, for thou art holy.

Miniſter.

and Merciful; Above all we praiſe thee, we worſhip thee, as the LORD GOD gracious and merciful; the GOD of love, and of all conſolation: thou exerciſeſt loving-kindneſs and benignity: thou delighteſt to make all thy creatures happy: thou doeſt good continually; and thy tender mercies are over all thy works.

People.

EVENING SERVICE.

People.

O that men would praise the LORD for his goodness, and for his wonderful works to the children of men.

Minister.

But who, O LORD, can shew forth all thy praise! we behold the monuments of thy power; we trace the footsteps of thy wisdom; and every moment of our lives partake of the riches of thy goodness; but none can say, how great, and wise, and good thou art.

People.

Who can find out thee, the almighty, unto perfection!

Minister.

With one consent, and with our whole hearts, we would celebrate thy glorious perfections here below, until our souls grow up to a due preparation for thy kingdom and service above; there to worship thee in a more perfect manner, through the ages of eternity. Amen. *and will celebrate his Perfections for ever.*

¶ *Here*

¶ *Here the* First Lesson *is to be read out of the* Holy Scriptures; *after which the* Service *is to proceed with the following* Thanksgiving, *the congregation standing.*

Minister.

"REJOICE in the LORD, all ye
"people: come into his presence with
"thanksgiving; and be devout and joyful in his service. Sing praises unto
"him, and bless him; for he is good,
"and his mercy endureth for ever."

People.

We will give thanks unto the LORD; *and celebrate his goodness with joyful hearts.*

Minister.

General Act of Thanksgiving.
ALMIGHTY GOD, Father of mercies; we would offer unto thee our unfeigned thanksgivings for the discoveries thou hast made of thyself in the works of thy hands; and for thy goodness and loving-kindness to us, and to all men. We

EVENING SERVICE.

We thank thee for our creation; for the excellent form of our bodies; for the breath of life; the light of reason, and conscience; the benevolent and friendly affections; and all the noble and useful powers of our minds. *for Creation; and Powers of Body, and Mind,*

We thank thee for our continual preservation; for the food we eat; the raiment with which we are cloathed; the habitations wherein we dwell; for capacity and ability to perform the duties of our stations; for health and peace, to enjoy the blessings of thy providence; for our present safety; and the opportunity we now enjoy of expressing, in this public manner, the grateful sentiments of our minds. *Preservation, and Blessings of Life.*

We thank thee for peaceable times, and healthful and fruitful seasons; for the administration of wise and equal laws; for the continuance of our liberties, both civil

vil and religious; for every personal and family blessing; for every friendly and social enjoyment; and for all the agreeable and happy circumstances of our lives.

People.

These are the gifts of thy bounty; thy name be praised for ever.

Minister.

Redemption by JESUS CHRIST, But above all we bless thee, O ever gracious Father, for thine inestimable love in the redemption of the world, by our LORD JESUS CHRIST; for the means of grace, and the hopes of glory. We thank thee for those pure and heavenly doctrines which he hath taught, to lead mankind in the way of truth, and salvation; for those holy and excellent rules of virtue and true religion, which he hath laid down in his gospel; and for the amiable and perfect example which he hath left us, that we might follow his steps.

EVENING SERVICE.

steps. We thank thee, that in obedience to thine authority, and to fulfil all righteousness, he submitted unto death; that being made perfect by suffering, he might become the Author of eternal salvation to all who obey him. *his Death,*

And finally we bless thee, the GOD and Father of our LORD JESUS CHRIST, that by raising him from the dead, thou hast confirmed to us the glorious and rejoicing hope of an inheritance incorruptible, undefiled, and which fadeth not away, reserved in the heavens for us. *and Resurrection.*

People.
Glory be to GOD in the highest; on earth peace; good will to men.

Minister.
O LORD our GOD, who can number all thy mercies! thy bounty prevents our requests; seasonably supplies every returning want, and gives us all things richly

richly to enjoy. Write a law of thankfulness on our hearts, we beseech thee, and grant that we may walk before thee, in holiness and righteousness, all the days of our lives. *Amen.*

¶ *Here a* Psalm of Praise, *or* Thanksgiving, *is to be sung; and after that the* Second Lesson *read, out of the* NEW TESTAMENT, *except on the* first Sunday *in the Month, when the* Ten Commandments, *and our Saviour's* Summary of the Moral Law, *are to be read, instead of the* Second Lesson, *in the* Evening Service; *for which purpose they are printed together after the* Occasional Forms.

¶ *Then the* Service *must proceed with the following* Address *to the People.*

Minister.

" SURELY it is meet to be said
" unto GOD we have done iniquity.
" To the LORD our GOD belong
" mercies and forgiveness, though we
" have sinned against him:
" Let

EVENING SERVICE. 53

" Let us therefore confefs and lament
" our manifold tranfgreffions, before the
" throne of the heavenly grace."

¶ *The* GENERAL CONFESSION; *to be read by the Minifter alone, the People kneeling.*

ALMIGHTY and moft merciful Father, we confefs that in many things we have all offended: we have not behaved as thy children, and as the difciples of our bleffed Saviour: we have not duly improved the talents with which thou haft intrufted us: we have too often neglected our duty to ourfelves, and to our fellow men; and our confciences witnefs againft us. With humble and penitent hearts, we lament before thee, O our Father, every inftance of difobedience; whatever we have done amifs in thought, word, or deed; every offence againft thee, our neighbour, or ourfelves: and if we have been injurious, unjuft, or have dealt deceitfully; if we have forgotten thy great loving-kindnefs, kindness, and departed from our character as men, and as christians, forgive us, according to thy promises by CHRIST JESUS our LORD; forgive our sins, we beseech thee, and cleanse us from all unrighteousness: and may we bring forth the fruits which are meet for repentance, by walking in newness of life, and studying to abound in holiness, and every good work. *Amen.*

¶ *Then the following* Prayers *are to be read by the Minister alone, the congregation still kneeling, and saying* Amen, *at the conclusion of each* Prayer.

A Prayer for the Pardon of Sin.

Minister.

O LORD GOD, whose nature is to have mercy, and to forgive, behold with compassion thy penitent creatures. Thou knowest our frame; thou remembrest that we are but dust: be merciful unto us, O GOD, be merciful unto us: may thy goodness lead us to repent-

repentance; to destroy every evil inclination and habit, and to form our minds to a virtuous and heavenly temper. May we have a fixed abhorrence of sin; and hereafter live soberly, righteously, and piously in this world, in humble expectation of thy mercy unto eternal life, declared to mankind by CHRIST JESUS, our LORD. *Amen.*

A Prayer founded on the Perfections of GOD.

O GOD, the unchangeable, and everlasting fountain of life, perfection, and happiness; we lift up our hearts unto thee, the greatest, wisest, and best of beings: from the contemplation of thy works, may we daily increase in the knowledge of thee; attain to more pure and worthy conceptions of thy nature, and providence; and ever manifest a becoming reverence for thy perfections; and a just concern for thine honour and service. Under a due sense of thine almighty power, we would avoid thy displeasure,

pleasure, as the worst of evils: from a full persuasion that thou art wise in counsel, faithful in thy promises, and righteous in all thy ways, we repose an unreserved confidence in all the measures of thy providence: as a being perfectly good, we would love thee with all our hearts, and rejoice in thine universal government. Above all we desire to yield a chearful obedience to thy commandments; and by the persevering love and practice of righteousness, in this world, we humbly pray that we may at length be prepared for thy glorious worship in the heavenly world above. *Amen.*

A Prayer respecting relative Duties.

O GOD, who art love, and who dwellest in love; may we earnestly endeavour to imitate thy constant and universal goodness: may we behave in our several stations with integrity and benevolence; and discover the true spirit of piety and goodness in all the relations of life: may we walk within our houses with

with perfect hearts; be faithful and affectionate to our friends; and just and charitable to all men: may we put on the ornament of a meek, compassionate, and forgiving spirit; and may every good and generous disposition be daily improving in our breasts, until we become fit for that happy kingdom, where love, and peace, and joy reign for evermore. *Amen.*

Self-government, and the personal Virtues.

O GOD of wisdom, teach us the knowledge of ourselves; may we keep our hearts with all diligence; and amidst the trials and changes of this world, maintain a constant habit of self-government: in prosperity may we be humble, temperate, and charitable; remembering that we are men: in adversity may we be patient, and wholly resigned to thine unerring providence. Save us, O gracious GOD, from anger and malice; from revenge and unchari-tableness;

tableness; from pride and presumption; from the snares of the wicked, and the fatal influence of every evil example: give us prudence to direct our affairs; resolution to preserve our innocence; and wisdom and constancy to retain our integrity as long as we live. *Amen.*

A Prayer relating to temporal Mercies.

ALMIGHTY GOD, the giver of every good and perfect gift, we recommend ourselves, and all our concerns to the disposal of thy gracious providence: thou knowest what is truly good for us; and it is our highest happiness that we are under thy fatherly care: in humble submission to thy wise and gracious will, we beseech thee to continue to us the use of our understanding, and reason; to bless us with health of body, and peace of mind; and to bestow upon us such a share of the good things of this life, as thou knowest to be best for us: conduct us by thy gracious hand through all the changes.

changes of this world; and may we at last be perfect and happy, in that heavenly inheritance, which is incorruptible and fadeth not away. *Amen.*

A Prayer for all Mankind.

O GOD, the Father of all mankind, we offer up unto thee our prayers and intercessions for our brethren, and fellow creatures, wherever dispersed: mercifully regard the work of thine hands: let thy name be known, and thy pure worship prevail throughout the world: may all people, nations, and languages acknowledge thee, the true GOD: put an end to idolatry, superstition, and all false religion; and especially to persecution for conscience sake: may wisdom and goodness, liberty and peace, charity and happiness, every where abound; and thy kingdom of truth and righteousness spread and flourish, until it cover the face of the whole earth. *Amen.*

For our native Country.

O ALMIGHTY and everlasting GOD, whose kingdom ruleth over all, we humbly beseech thee to continue thy protection and favour to our native country, and all the dominions thereunto belonging: may true religion prevail; public liberty be established; an effectual stop be put to the progress of error, injustice, profaneness, and all immorality; and may truth, righteousness, and charity, abound more and more. If it seemeth good to thy perfect wisdom, graciously preserve us from pestilence and famine; and from all the wasting calamities of war: may peace be within our walls, and prosperity within our cities; and may all the privileges we enjoy, be secured to us, and handed down to the latest posterity. *Amen.*

For the King.

O LORD GOD, high and mighty king of kings, and lord of lords, send down thy heavenly blessings upon thy servant GEORGE, our rightful sovereign: preserve his life and health: may he be eminent for wisdom, and the virtues becoming his high station; may he be the faithful guardian of our public liberties; and the happy instrument of transmitting them to posterity: may his reign be long and prosperous; and may he finally be rewarded with immortal glory and felicity. *Amen.*

For the Queen, and the Royal Family.

O GOD, the Author of all good, bless our gracious Queen CHARLOTTE, the Prince of WALES, the Princess Dowager of WALES, and all the Royal Family: may thy watchful providence evermore defend them from all evil, and prosper them with all good: guide them by thy counsel in this world, and

EVENING SERVICE.

and afterwards receive them into thine everlasting kingdom. *Amen.*

For the Parliament.
[*To be read only when sitting.*]

O GOD, the fountain of all wisdom, and the disposer of all events, be graciously present in the great council of the nation, at this time in parliament assembled: may they have wisdom to discern, and integrity to pursue the welfare of these kingdoms: and may all their debates be so over-ruled by thy gracious governance, as finally to terminate in thy honour; the encouragement of virtue, and true religion; and the establishment of our public liberties throughout all generations. *Amen.*

For Privy Counsellors, Nobility, Judges, Magistrates, and all the People.

MAY it please thee, O GOD, who hast the hearts of all men in thine hands, to bless the King's privy coun-

counsellors, the nobility, judges, magistrates, and the whole body of the people of this land: may they all discharge the duties of their stations with fidelity and good conscience; severally contribute to the general welfare and happiness; and thus be prepared for thine approbation, and acceptance unto eternal life. *Amen.*

For Christian Ministers.

O GOD, the Father of our LORD JESUS CHRIST, the fountain of light, from whom cometh every good and perfect gift, we humbly beseech thee to send down thy heavenly blessing upon Christian ministers, of every denomination: may they be so replenished with the truth of thy doctrine; and so exemplary in unaffected piety and goodness of life, that they may become the happy means of turning many to righteousness; and of promoting the knowledge and practice of the pure and holy Gospel of JESUS CHRIST, our LORD. *Amen.*

For the afflicted.

O GOD, the Creator and Preserver of mankind, we commend to thy fatherly goodness, all those who are any-ways afflicted or distressed in mind, body, or estate; [*especially those for whom our prayers are desired;*] may it please thee to comfort and relieve them according to their several necessities; giving them patience under their sufferings; and a happy issue out of all their afflictions. *Amen.*

Concluding Prayer.

O LORD GOD, our heavenly Father, who hast permitted us with one accord to make our common supplications unto thee, fulfil, we beseech thee, the desires and petitions of thy servants, as thou in thy wisdom knowest to be good for us: we commit ourselves to the care of thy providence: mercifully defend us from all the dangers to which we may be exposed: graciously accept

EVENING SERVICE.

accept thefe our fervices; and grant that in all our works begun, continued, and ended, we may glorify thy holy name; and finally obtain everlafting life and felicity; which we humbly pray for in the name, and as the difciples of JESUS CHRIST, our LORD; in whofe words we conclude our prayers for ourfelves, and for all mankind:

OUR Father, who art in heaven; hallowed be thy name: thy kingdom come: thy will be done on earth as it is in heaven: give us this day our daily bread; forgive us our trefpaffes, as we forgive thofe who trefpafs againft us; lead us not into temptation; but deliver us from evil: for thine is the kingdom, the power, and the glory, for ever and ever. *Amen.*

¶ *Here a* Pfalm *is to be fung, while the Minifter is preparing for the pulpit.*

¶ *The* Benediction *is to be pronounced by the Minifter, at the conclufion of the whole Service.*

THE
THIRD SERVICE;

¶ *To be used either Morning, or Evening, at the choice of the Minister.*

¶ *This* Service *is to be introduced by the following* Prayer, *the Congregation rising up.*

¶ *The* Introductory Prayer; *to be read by the Minister alone.*

INFINITELY great, most glorious, and ever blessed LORD, our GOD! The heavens, and the earth, and all things which we behold, shew forth thy existence, and declare thy perfections. Thy goodness is unchangeable, and thy wisdom past finding out. Thou art exalted

THE THIRD SERVICE.

alted in majesty and power, far above our highest conceptions; yet thou regardest us with the tenderness of a Father, and shewest favour, and loving-kindness to the children of men. We would now offer up unto thee, O GOD, our religious addresses, encouraged by thy goodness, and the gracious promises in the Gospel of thy Son. May we remember thee our Creator, Preserver, and Benefactor, with fear, love, and gratitude; and worship thee, who art a spirit, in spirit and in truth; that our various services may be acceptable in thy sight, and truly beneficial to our own souls. May we hearken to the reading of thy word, as to the voice of GOD; sing thy praises with understanding and devotion; and hear what shall be delivered for our instruction, with attention, candour and humility; that by all the means of grace, we may grow wiser and better; be gradually trained up for thy heavenly kingdom; and at last become partakers of that happiness, which

which eye hath not seen, which ear hath not heard, and which it hath not entered into the heart of man to conceive.------ These our petitions we present unto thee, in the name, and as the disciples of our LORD and Saviour JESUS CHRIST. *Amen.*

¶ *Then the following* HYMN, *for celebrating the* DIVINE PERFECTIONS, *is to be recited by the Minister and People, alternately, all standing.*

Minister.

We celebrate the divine Perfections of
WE praise thee, O GOD, we acknowledge and adore thee, the one, true, and living GOD, who alone art independent and eternal; whose perfections are infinite, and counsels unchangeable; the greatest, wisest, and best of beings; the confidence and joy of

of all those to whom thou hast made thyself known.

By thy power were the heavens created; and all their hosts by the breath of thy mouth: thy hand preserveth them in being; they are the ministers of thy good pleasure. *Power,*

Thou disposest all things in perfect wisdom; and maintainest the beauty and order of thy works: all creatures are subject to thy direction; and thou assignest them their proper station and duty. *Wisdom,*

With the highest veneration, we present our addresses to thee, a Being of almighty power, and unerring wisdom: but in an especial manner do we acknowledge, with unfeigned love, and joyful confidence, thine infinite and everlasting goodness: thou art the fountain of happiness; and thou diffusest thy blessings through all the works of thy hands. The heavens *and Goodness:*

heavens declare thy glory; the earth is full of thy goodnefs: the day is thine, the night alfo is thine; and thou makeft the morning, and the evening to rejoice.

All the works of thy hands, and all the ordinances of thy providence, bear teftimony that thou art infinitely great, and wife, and good.

The higheft and moft exalted angels adore thee, O LORD, who art good, and doeft good continually; who art wife in heart, wonderful in counfel, and excellent in working.

We, thine intelligent creatures in this world, join our tribute of joyful praife to thee, O GOD, the fovereign Creator and LORD of all: thou alone art worthy to receive glory, and honour, and praife, from all thy creatures. " Praife " ye the LORD."

People.

O GOD, thy perfections fill our hearts with love and joy: and our lips fhew forth thy praife.

Minifter.

THE THIRD SERVICE.

Minister.

"O magnify the LORD with me, and let us bless his name together." Thou, O GOD, art the Creator of mankind; thy hands have made us, and fashioned us; thou hast cloathed us with skin and flesh, and fenced us with sinews and bones. Thou hast created the spirit that is in man; breathed into us the breath of life; and, by thine inspiration, hast given us understanding.

We bless the LORD; who is our

Creator.

People.

O GOD, thou hast made us, and not we ourselves; we are thy people, and the sheep of thy pasture.

Minister.

Thou, O GOD, art the Giver of life: in thy hand is the soul of every living thing, and the breath of all mankind: thou art the Preserver of men.

Preserver.

People.

THE THIRD SERVICE.

People.

Thy visitation preserveth our spirits; and thou, LORD, makest us to dwell in safety.

Minister.

Governor, O thou most high GOD, Possessor of heaven and earth, the Judge of all, and the universal King; thy government is righteous; thy providence perfect; and all thy commandments are holy, just, and good: the obedience of all reasonable creatures is due to thee alone, the King of kings, the Lord of lords, the blessed and only Potentate.

People.

We bow ourselves before thee, thy willing subjects; thy commandments are true, and righteous altogether.

Minister.

and common Father; O GOD, thou art our Creator, and righteous Governor; we rejoice in the being we have received from thee; we yield a willing sub-

THE THIRD SERVICE.

submission to all the orders of thy government; and we address thee as our Father, who hast made us to bear thine image, and to partake of the blessings of thy family.

People.
We are thy children; therefore do we pray unto thee.

Minister.
We rejoice in thy fatherly care, which thou hast manifested to us, ever since we came into the world.

People.
We put our confidence in thee, whose counsel is our guide; and whose favour is our highest happiness.

Minister.
Now unto thee, the king eternal, immortal, and invisible, the only wise, living, and true GOD, we ascribe our chearful and united praises. *Amen.* <small>and to him we ascribe our united Praises.</small>

¶ *Here*

THE THIRD SERVICE.

¶ *Here the* first Lesson *is to be read out of the* HOLY SCRIPTURES; *after which the* Service *is to proceed with the following* THANKSGIVING, *the congregation rising up.*

Minister.

General Thanksgiving:

EVER gracious and most merciful Father, we render unto thee our sincere thanks for the manifold mercies we are continually receiving from thy hands; and we desire to recollect them with sentiments of religious gratitude; and with hearty purposes to act agreeably to them.

for Creation,

O GOD, thou art the Giver of all good; thou delightest in the happiness of thy creatures, and art daily imparting the riches of thy bounty. We thank thee, especially, for all the instances of thy goodness to ourselves. Thou art the Former of our bodies, and the Father of our spirits. Thou hast

THE THIRD SERVICE.

haſt exerciſed a wiſe and gracious care over us, ever ſince we came into the world: by thee are all our wants ſupplied; from thee all our enjoyments proceed; and thou crowneſt our days with thy goodneſs. We bleſs thee, who giveſt us food convenient for us, and appointeſt refreſhment for our wearied powers. To thy kind and merciful providence we owe the raiment with which we are cloathed; our comfortable habitations; and all the fruits of our induſtry and labour. *Preſervation, and Bleſſings of Life:*

We thank thee for reaſon and underſtanding; and for all the treaſures of knowledge thou haſt opened to our view; that thou haſt formed us for the practice of virtue, and true religion; and given us many opportunities for the improvement of our minds, and the attainment of our higheſt happineſs. *for Powers of the Mind and Means of Improvement;*

THE THIRD SERVICE.

for social Affections, We thank thee, that we are placed in a social state; are endued with social affections; and enjoy such a variety of pleasures, from the esteem and friendship of our brethren.

Pleasures of Wisdom & Virtue; and Prospect of a happier State. To thy goodness we ascribe all the enjoyments we receive from the practice of virtue, and the just exercise of our powers; the variety of trials thou hast appointed for the improvement and perfection of our natures here; and the prospect thou givest us of a more perfect and happy state hereafter. " O give thanks unto the LORD, " for he is good, and his mercies " endure for ever."

People.

We give thanks unto the LORD, for he is good, and his mercies endure for ever.

Minister.

For the various Dispensations of Providence, We bless thee, thou wise and gracious Disposer of all things, for the various dispensations of thy

THE THIRD SERVICE.

thy providence in favour of religion, and the happiness of mankind, in the several ages of the world; for all the divine messengers thou hast sent; by whose instructions and example, thy light and truth have been preserved, in the darkest times of ignorance and idolatry. *in favour of Religion,*

Above all, we thank thee, merciful Father, for the display of the exceeding riches of thy goodness in CHRIST JESUS; by whom thou hast made every necessary provision, for our improvement in the knowledge and practice of true religion. *for JESUS CHRIST;*

Blessed be thy name, O GOD, for this divine teacher, and Saviour, whom thou hast sent to declare unto us thy heavenly will; to save us from ignorance and vice; and to lead us, by his heavenly instructions, and amiable example, to the love and practice of universal goodness.

We

We offer up our moſt joyful gratitude to thee, the GOD and Father of our LORD JESUS CHRIST, that by him we are aſſured of pardon, and thy gracious acceptance, upon our return to obedience and virtue; that he has opened before us the ſolemnities of a future judgment; and confirmed to us the joyful hope of glory, honour, and immortality. "O give thanks unto the LORD, "for he is good, and his mercies "endure for ever."

People.

Bleſſed be the GOD, and Father of our LORD JESUS CHRIST; for he is good, and his mercies endure for ever.

Miniſter.

and the Reformation. We thank thee, heavenly Father, that though the pure and holy religion of JESUS was corrupted by wicked men, and its divine light darkened, in thine own due time a reformation was brought

THE THIRD SERVICE.

brought about, under the direction of thy wife providence; and that we now enjoy our christian liberty, and christian privileges, in peace and tranquillity; none being permitted to rise up, and make us afraid. " O give thanks to " the GOD of heaven, for his mercy " endureth for ever."

People.
Blessed be the LORD our GOD, for he is good, and his mercy endureth for ever.

¶ *Here a* Psalm of Praise, *or* Thanksgiving, *is to be sung; and after that the* Second Lesson *read, out of the* NEW TESTAMENT, *except when this* Service *is used for the* Evening *of the* first Sunday *in the Month; and then the* Ten Commandments, *together with our Saviour's* Summary *of the* Moral Law, *are to be read, instead of the* Second Lesson; *for which purpose they are placed at the end of the* Occasional Forms.

¶ *Then*

¶ *Then muſt the Miniſter read the following* Confession, *the Miniſter and People all kneeling.*

THE GENERAL CONFESSION.

ALMIGHTY and moſt merciful Father, we confeſs that we have often ſinned againſt thee: we have diſregarded thine authority, and abuſed thy goodneſs: we have left undone thoſe things which we ought to have done; and done thoſe things which we ought not to have done: we have acted inconſiſtently with our chriſtian character; and departed from the holy commandment delivered unto us: we have been unmindful of the perfect example ſet before us; and forgotten the ſure and precious promiſes to which we are called: our only hope is in thy mercy: on thy mercy thou haſt encouraged us to hope; and haſt declared by thy Son CHRIST JESUS, that if we return to the obedience of thy commandments, thou wilt have mercy, and forgive us.

People.

THE THIRD SERVICE.

People.

To the LORD *our* GOD *belong mercies and forgiveness, though we have sinned against him.*

¶ *Then the following* Prayers *are to be read by the Minister alone, the Congregation still kneeling, and saying* Amen, *at the conclusion of each* Prayer.

A Prayer for Forgiveness.

O LORD GOD, who delightest in mercy, and art not willing that any should perish, but that all should repent and live; suffer us not to perish in our transgressions; and save us especially from the dominion of them, for the time to come. Vouchsafe unto us the light of thy countenance; and establish our minds with a sense of thy approbation, and the hopes of thy favour and acceptance unto eternal life. *Amen.*

For divine Assistance.

O GOD, the Author of all good, grant us, we beseech thee, thy gracious assistance in the future course of our lives; and teach us to act agreeably to the profession we make, and the desires we have now expressed before thee. Give us such a deep persuasion of the evil of sin, and of the importance and excellency of a holy and virtuous life, that we may carefully abstain from all iniquity, and be filled with the fruits of righteousness, which are to thy honour and glory. *Amen.*

For the Knowledge and Improvement of religious Truth.

O MERCIFUL GOD, who art the Father of lights, and fountain of all wisdom; enlighten our minds with the knowledge of all useful truths; may they sink deep into our hearts, and influence our whole conduct. Having a steadfast faith in thy perfections, may we act

act with integrity, and order our whole converſation as in thy ſight; may we preſerve a conſtant regard to thy perfect adminiſtration; and receive with ſubmiſſion and chearfulneſs whatever thou appointeſt: by the knowledge of thee, who alone art good, may we improve in the love of goodneſs; and may the hope we are encouraged to entertain, of thy continual ſupport and aſſiſtance, animate us in the practice of all good works. May the manifeſtation of thy mercy to mankind by JESUS CHRIST, awaken our averſion to ſin; engage us to excel in every virtue; and conſtantly to purſue, what thou, the righteous Judge, approveſt, and wilt finally reward and honour. By a diligent attention to the truths of our moſt holy religion, may our minds be purified from all corrupt and ſenſual paſſions; may we acquire a more perfect command over ourſelves; proceed after the example of JESUS, in the practice of all goodneſs, and never be weary of well doing: and above all, by the expectation of an happy immortality, may our virtue be supported, and our peace secured, until we are removed from the present, to a higher state of being; and become partakers of that everlasting happiness, which thou hast promised to thy faithful servants. *Amen.*

For the Practice of particular Duties.

O GRACIOUS GOD, from whom all holy and good desires do proceed, produce in our minds those sentiments which may dispose us to all the duties of life; that in humility and meekness we may walk before thee; and being content with such things as we have, may leave all future events to thy gracious appointment. Incline us to thy worship and service, and all the offices of piety to thee, our Father in heaven. Teach us to enjoy the gifts of thy bounty with thankfulness; and to pass thro' the afflictions, thou appointest for us, with patience and submission to thy holy will.

THE THIRD SERVICE. 85

Assist us in the discharge of all social, and relative duties: may we be honest in all our dealings; and delight in doing good: may we be ready to relieve the poor, and to shew compassion to all who are in distress: may we be grateful to our friends; forgive our enemies; and always do to others, as we would they should do to us.

Establish in our souls a prevailing desire to bear a nearer resemblance to thee, the original of all perfection; and to be in a state of continual improvement, and preparation for the felicities which thou hast provided for all good men, from the foundation of the world.

And grant, O merciful Father, that by thus expressing before thee, the desires of our hearts, we may be more determined to live after thy commandments; and so attain that peace of mind, which is thy peculiar gift; and after a comfortable and happy life, be advanced to thine everlasting kingdom. *Amen.*

THE THIRD SERVICE.

A Prayer respecting external Things.

O GOD, our heavenly Father, to the direction of thy wise and unerring providence we do entirely commit ourselves: safe under thy protection, and happy in thy favour, we would chearfully follow, where thou pleasest to conduct us: we desire only that portion of the good things of this life, which thou seest to be fit for us; and would decline no sufferings, which thou shalt appoint, for the trial and improvement of our virtue: save us, we beseech thee, from the snares of prosperity and adversity: suffer us not to forget thee in our abundance; or to question thy goodness in our distress: in health, and in sickness, in life and in death, may we lift up our souls unto thee; and make thy goodness alone our confidence and joy: and may we so pass through the changing scenes of the present world, that we may be prepared for the pure and unmixed happiness of thy glorious presence for evermore. *Amen.*

For all Mankind.

O GOD, the Father of all mankind, we rejoice in thine universal providence; and, with full confidence, commit to thy direction all the circumstances of our fellow creatures. Thou art the fountain of all blessings; thou delightest in doing good: grant, merciful Father, that all mankind may perceive thy hand in the advantages they enjoy; and be disposed to render thee their humble thanks, for all the instances of thy beneficence: and by their gratitude to thee, may their good dispositions be improved, and their happiness increased continually. *Amen.*

For all Christian Churches.

WE beseech thee, O GOD of love and mercy, to send down thy blessing upon all who profess the faith of our LORD JESUS CHRIST: suffer not their divisions to injure the cause of of truth and liberty: graciously assist those who love thy holy name, in all their sincere endeavours to reform the abuses which have entered into thy church; and to promote the peace and union of Christians: give them just sentiments of the nature, and tendency of our holy religion: fill their hearts with love to thee, and to each other; may they approve themselves the faithful disciples of JESUS; and become the instruments of diffusing virtue and happiness in the world. *Amen*

For the Advancement of Christian Knowledge.

O LORD, who would'st have all men to be saved, fill the minds of thy reasonable creatures with the knowledge of thy truth: cause thy light to shine upon those who sit in darkness; dispel the prejudices under which they labour: above all, we beg that thou would'st deliver them from every evil affection; and bring them into the way of of truth, and happiness. May the Gospel of JESUS prevail through the world; and by the power of its truth, and the exemplary conduct of those who profess it, enter the hearts and govern the lives of all the inhabitants of the earth; and make all the nations righteous and happy. *Amen.*

For the civil Happiness of Mankind.

LORD GOD, who ruleth in the nations, reform, we beseech thee, all the disorders which arise from the evil passions of men: [put a stop to the wasting calamities of war;] and prosper the just designs of all those who delight in peace: may the blessings of free and equal government become universal: and under the influence of good laws, and a righteous administration, may all the advantages of civil society be widely extended; and the best interests of mankind effectually secured: and whilst thy creatures enjoy the gifts of thy bounty, may they unite in praise and thanksgiving to thee, the Author of all good. *Amen.*

For our own Country.

WE commit to thee, our righteous Governor, all the important interests of our native Country: grant, we beseech thee, that we may live in safety; and enjoy the blessings thy providence has bestowed upon us, in tranquillity and peace: mercifully preserve us from all public calamities: and that we may escape the destructive evils which thou appointest for wicked nations, may we be disposed to a general reformation of manners; and may true religion and virtue so prevail amongst us, that our tranquillity may be continued, and our distinguished privileges be handed down to succeeding ages. Bless all our colonies: prosper our alliance with foreign nations: give us the fruits of the earth in their seasons; and may our trade and commerce be so conducted, as to become

become inftruments of good to the whole nation. Vouchfafe thy favour to all orders of men among us: by a diligent and chearful difcharge of the duties of their feveral ftations, may they contribute their part to the public welfare, and the happinefs of all mankind. Beftow upon us, O merciful Father, every thing truly good; and may we with one heart, acknowledge and praife thee, who art good, and doeft good continually. *Amen.*

For the King.

WE recommend to the care of thy providence, thy fervant GEORGE our King: fill his heart with every royal virtue; and affift him in the important duties to which he is called: preferve him from the defigns of his enemies; give him the hearts of all his fubjects; and by their fidelity and zeal, may his ufeful defigns be encouraged, and promoted: fucceed his juft undertakings; and after a life of great and extenfive ufefulnefs in this world, advance him to thy heavenly and everlasting kingdom. *Amen.*

For the Queen, and Royal Family.

MAY it please thee to bless our gracious Queen CHARLOTTE; the Prince of WALES; the Princess Dowager of WALES; and all the Royal Family: by the influence of a good example, and a wise and faithful discharge of the duties of their high stations, may they become great and extensive blessings: may their happiness increase continually in this world; and in the future state be crowned with immortal glory. *Amen.*

For the Parliament, when sitting.

BLESS, we beseech thee, the high court of Parliament; may all the members of that great assembly be men fearing thee, and hating covetousness: preside in their counsels; prosper their good designs; and may they wisely discern, and steadily pursue the true interests of these kingdoms. *Amen.*

THE THIRD SERVICE.

For the Nobility and Gentry.

BLESS the nobility, and gentry, and all who are in stations of authority and power; may they employ all their influence to promote righteousness and virtue; become the means of diffusing public and private blessings; and be faithful stewards of the manifold bounties of thy providence. *Amen.*

For Judges and Magistrates.

BLESS our judges and magistrates; may they dispense justice with impartiality; discountenance profaneness and vice; and be an encouragement and praise to all who do well. *Amen.*

For Christian Ministers.

WE recommend to thy gracious regard the ministers of the christian religion; humbly beseeching thee, that their faithful endeavours to extend the knowledge of thy truth, and to promote

mote the love and practice of thy holy commandments, may be favourably accepted, and become succefsful: may they do honour to thy truth, in their public fervices, and in their lives; and do thou direct thy fervants, in the way of righteoufnefs, to their highest happinefs. *Amen.*

For rich and poor.

BLESS those who are rich in this world, with a difpofition to do good: may the poor be fober, honeft, and diligent in their ftations, and confide in thy providence; and may we all be thankful to thee for the bleffings thou art pleafed to beftow upon us. *Amen.*

For the afflicted.

O GOD of mercy, we humbly beg thy favourable regard to all our brethren in affliction: may thy wifdom be their direction; thy power their fupport; and thy goodnefs their confidence; and, by a patient behaviour under

THE THIRD SERVICE.

under their afflictions, and a thankful acknowledgment of all thy mercies, may they be prepared for unmixed happiness, in a future and better world. *Amen.*

A general Prayer.

MERCIFULLY regard, O heavenly Father, these our petitions for ourselves, and for others; continue to us such measures of the good things of this life, as thou seest to be best for us: may thy good providence defend us thro' this [day,] *or* [night,] and through all the future days and nights of our lives; teach us the right use of all our enjoyments; lead us to a wise and careful improvement of all thy mercies; and finally advance us to thy glorious and everlasting kingdom. *Amen.*

A concluding Prayer.

O GOD, the Father of mercies, and the Father of our LORD JESUS CHRIST, we humbly offer to thy gracious acceptance these our prayers, in his

his name: we rejoice that thou haſt raiſed him above men and angels; that thou haſt given him a kingdom; and that by him thou haſt promiſed to beſtow immortal life and happineſs upon all thy faithful ſervants: by his inſtructions and example we deſire to govern our lives; and in his form of words we conclude our prayers to thee,

OUR Father, who art in heaven; hallowed be thy name: thy kingdom come: thy will be done on earth as it is in heaven: give us this day our daily bread; forgive us our treſpaſſes, as we forgive thoſe who treſpaſs againſt us; lead us not into temptation; but deliver us from evil: for thine is the kingdom, the power, and the glory, for ever and ever. *Amen.*

¶ *Here a* Pſalm *is to be ſung, while the Miniſter is preparing for the pulpit.*

¶ *The* Benediction *muſt be pronounced by the Miniſter, at the concluſion of the* whole Service.

OCCASIONAL PRAYERS

AND

THANKSGIVINGS;

¶ *To be made use of as the Minister shall think proper.*

OCCASIONAL PRAYERS.

A Collect adapted to the Spring Season.

O LORD, the Creator, and Preserver of all things, who with unerring wisdom maintainest the beauty and order of thy works; we look up with joy and confidence unto thy gracious power, which causes the returning seasons to know their place: thou hast sent forth thy spirit; thou hast renewed

OCCASIONAL PRAYERS.

the face of the earth: bless, we beseech thee, the springing of the year; and enrich the earth with the rain of heaven: may grass grow for the cattle, and herbs and fruits for the service of man; may our pastures be cloathed with flocks; our vallies covered with corn; and the year crowned with thy goodness: and may we so improve the various blessings of thy providence in this world, as to be prepared for the unchangeable felicities of thine everlasting kingdom. *Amen.*

A Collect adapted to the Season of Harvest.

ALMIGHTY GOD, the Fountain of all goodness, in whose power alone it is to give fruitful seasons, and to fill our hearts with food and gladness; we lift up our eyes unto thee, from whom our hope cometh, beseeching thee to preserve unto us the appointed weeks of harvest, and to give us seasonable weather for ripening, and gathering in the fruits of the earth, that in due time we we may enjoy them. * *May the immoderate rains be abated; and thy mercy again shine upon us.* Suffer not the hopes of the husbandman to fail; may the poor be satisfied with bread; continue to bless us with the bounties of thy providence; and may we evermore live to thy praise, in a wise, grateful, and temperate enjoyment of thy mercies, who art the only Giver of all good. Amen.

A Collect to be used on Occasion of any violent Storm, or Earthquake.

GREAT and glorious LORD GOD, almighty in thy power, and unsearchable in all thy ways, at whose rebuke the earth trembles, and the foundations of the hills do shake; who thundereft with thy voice, and sendest forth thy lightnings to the ends of the heavens; who commandest the winds, and the sea, and they obey; we, the children of men, prostrate ourselves before thy

---

* *Only to be read in such a season as is there referred to.*

thy throne, adoring the greatnefs of thy majefty, and imploring thy favour and mercy to us. Awaken our attention duly to confider the voice of thy providence; and poffefs our hearts with a holy reverence of thy power, and a humble confidence in thy goodnefs. It is of thy goodnefs that we have not been confumed: in the midft of the amazing inftances of thy power, thou remembereft mercy; fhewing forth the care of thy providence in our prefervation. May the remembrance of thefe things produce in us thankfulnefs of heart, and fuch ferioufnefs of fpirit, that no calamity may ever furprife us, nor death it felf find us unprepared; and this we beg, for thy goodnefs fake, declared unto mankind by JESUS CHRIST our LORD. *Amen.*

OCCASIONAL PRAYERS.

A Collect to be read in Time of War.

O ALMIGHTY GOD, King of all kings, and Governor of all things, to whom it juſtly belongeth to puniſh ſinful nations, and to be merciful to thoſe, who repent; we humbly beſeech thee, in this time of our danger, to be the Defender of our country: give us not up into the hands of our enemies; ſave us from the edge of the ſword; and preſerve our land from the deſolations of war; continue us in the undiſturbed profeſſion of thy true religion; in the enjoyment of our public liberties; and may we yet live ſecure and happy, under that wiſe and equal government, which thou haſt ſet over us. We do with all humility acknowledge ourſelves unworthy of theſe peculiar bleſſings: have mercy upon us; O GOD, have mercy upon thy people: ſend forth a ſpirit of reformation amongſt us; avert the evils we have deſerved; continue thy favour and protection to us; ſave and deliver us, O our GOD, for in thee

do

OCCASIONAL PRAYERS.

do we put our trust: restore tranquillity and peace to contending nations; unite the hearts of mankind in the bonds of humanity and love; and may the happy time come, when the calamities of war shall cease for ever; and peace and righteousness universally prevail. And this we humbly beg, for thy mercy's sake, declared unto mankind by CHRIST JESUS our LORD. *Amen.*

A Collect to be used in a Time of remarkable Scarcity.

O GOD, our heavenly Father, by whose wise and gracious appointment it is, that the rain doth fall; the earth is fruitful; the beasts increase; and fishes do multiply; behold, we beseech thee, the present afflictions of thy people; alleviate the distresses of the miserable; and may the cries of the poor come unto thee: increase the fruits of the earth by thy heavenly benediction; may our scarcity be turned into plenty; and grant that we may improve the

the bounties of thy providence, to thy praife, in relieving the diftreffes of others; and by thankfully acknowledging thee, the Giver of every good and perfect gift. *Amen.*

A Collect adapted to a Time of general Sicknefs.

ALMIGHTY, and moft wife GOD, whofe never-failing providence ordereth all things both in heaven and in earth; we humbly direct our addreffes unto thee, in this time of our calamity, befeeching thee in behalf of our fellow creatures and friends, who are fuffering under the grievous ficknefs, with which thou art pleafed to vifit us: may the everlafting arms of thy mercy fupport them, and the confideration of thy fatherly goodnefs ftrengthen and comfort their fouls, in this time of their diftrefs: fanctify this general affliction to the reformation of our manners, and the improvement of our virtue; and caufe us to rejoice in the humble hope, that

that every thing shall work together for good. In the midst of life we are in death: of whom may we seek for succour, but of thee, O GOD: restrain the progress of the disorder, if it be agreeable to thy blessed will. May those lives that are yet spared be devoted to thy service; and may we, and all thy servants, be prepared for every event of thy Providence; that whether we live, we may live unto the LORD; or whether we die, we may die unto the LORD; and whether living or dying, may have an interest in thy mercies unto eternal life. *Amen.*

¶ *A Prayer for Women drawing near to the Time of Child-bearing.*

O GOD, the Author of life, the Fountain of happiness, and the gracious Preserver of those who do put their trust in thee, mercifully regard thy servants, who are drawing near to the time of child-bearing, and desire to recommend themselves to thy almighty
protec-

protection: save and deliver them in the hour of pain by thy gracious aid; may they be joyful mothers of living and perfect children; and in due time restore them to health and strength; that they may enter into thy gates with thanksgiving, and into thy courts with praise, be thankful unto thee, and bless thy Name. *Amen.*

A Prayer to be read, when particularly desired, for Persons upon Journies, or Voyages.

ALMIGHTY GOD, the Preserver of all thy creatures, and the Confidence of the ends of the earth, and of them who are afar off upon the seas; we humbly recommend to thy continual protection, such as are absent from their friends, upon journies in our own, or in foreign nations: may thy gracious providence defend them at all times, and in all places: preserve them from the peculiar dangers to which they may be exposed; succeed them in all

OCCASIONAL PRAYERS.

all their lawful and honourable defigns; and return them to their habitations in innocence and fafety, that they may have frefh occafions to celebrate the praifes of thy goodnefs with thankful hearts.----WE, in a particular manner, befeech thee in behalf of thy fervants, who are going down to the fea in fhips, or are now travelling upon the great ocean; O eternal LORD GOD, who commandeft the winds, and ruleft the raging of the waters, receive them under thine almighty and moft gracious protection; preferve them from the dangers of the fea, * *from the violence of the Enemy,* and the attempts of wicked and unreafonable men; return them to their native country in fafety, to enjoy the fruits of their induftry and labour; the benefits of fociety; and the pleafures of domeftic life; with a thankful remembrance of thy mercies, who art the only Giver of all good. *Amen.*

* *Only to be read in a time of war.*

OCCASIONAL THANKSGIVINGS.

A Thanksgiving for a plentiful Harvest.

ALMIGHTY and ever blessed GOD, who mercifully supplieth the wants of thy creatures, and art continually giving testimonies of thy gracious Providence; we rejoice at this time with humble thankfulness in the gifts of thine undeserved bounty; that thou hast caused the earth to yield its increase; ‡ *hast turned our scarcity into plenty*; and crowned the year with thy goodness: whilst thou art thus sending down thy blessings upon us, may we be disposed to live in a sober, temperate, and charitable enjoyment of them; and to bring forth the fruits of holiness, and righteousness, all the days of our lives. *Amen.*

‡ *Only to be read after a time of scarcity.*

OCCASIONAL THANKSGIVINGS.

For the Ceasing of a general Sickness, and the Restoration of the public Health.

WE thank thee, O GOD, our heavenly Father, that of thy great mercy thou hast assuaged the contagious sickness, with which our country has of late been visited; and hast in so good a measure restored the public health: in the midst of our afflictions thou hast remembred mercy; thou hast caused the voice of joy and gladness to be heard within our dwellings: we bless thy holy name for our preservation; and render unto thee, the GOD of all mercies, glory, and honour, thanksgiving and grateful praises now, and for evermore. *Amen.*

For public Peace, after a Time of War.

EVER gracious GOD, the Father of all mankind, and the Governor of all the nations of the earth, we give thee our unfeigned thanks, that it

OCCASIONAL THANKSGIVINGS.

it has pleafed thee to put a ftop to the dreadful calamities of war, and to unite the contending nations in the bonds of peace: we thank thee, that we have been delivered from the dangers to which we were expofed; that the public liberties of our country are preferved; and that we are ftill in poffeffion of many valuable priviledges and bleffings; continue to give peace in our time, O LORD; may the violent paffions of wicked men be reftrained; may the unjuft defigns of tyrants be difappointed; and may the happy time come, when the nations fhall learn war no more; and all mankind fhall be united in peace and love; and in the holy worfhip of thee, the true GOD, as the common difciples of JESUS CHRIST our LORD. *Amen.*

A Thankfgiving for Recovery from Sicknefs.

O LORD, our heavenly Father, who redeemeft the lives of thy fervant from deftruction; and giveft health, and life,

life, and blessing; accept the sincere and humble thanksgivings of thy servant, whom thou hast raised from a bed of sickness, and restored to some good measure of health and strength: we praise thee for this gracious instance of thy goodness: may the remembrance of thy late mercy to *him*, have a happy and lasting influence upon *his* mind: confirm and establish the good resolutions *he* has formed: and may that life, which thy mercy prolongs, be devoted to thy service, in a constant obedience to thy holy commandments. *Amen.*

A Thanksgiving for a Person's safe Return from a Journey, or Voyage.

ALMIGHTY GOD, the Preserver of all thy Creatures, and the Confidence of the ends of the earth, and of those who are afar off upon the seas; we offer up unto thee our united thanksgivings for the signal mercies thou hast vouchsafed to thy servant, whom thou hast preserved in *his* [*Journey*] or [*Voyage:*]

OCCASIONAL THANKSGIVINGS.

age:] that thou haſt protected *him* from every danger, to which *he* was expoſed; and haſt reſtored *him* to his friends in health, ſafety, and peace. Write a law of thankfulneſs upon *his* heart; and hereby engage *him* to a diligent and grateful obedience of all thy commandments. *Amen.*

A Thankſgiving for a Woman after Child-bearing.

ALMIGHTY GOD, the Father of all mercies, the GOD of all conſolation; we preſent before thee our unfeigned thanks, for thy great mercy vouchſafed to thy ſervant, here in thy preſence; whom thou haſt delivered from the pains and dangers of child-bearing; * *and made the living Mother of a living and perfect Child.* Thou haſt dealt gracioully with thy ſervant; haſt cauſed her ſorrow to be ſucceeded by joy; and anguiſh by refreſhment and eaſe: may a grateful remembrance of

* *Only to be read when the Child is living.*

OCCASIONAL THANKSGIVINGS.

of thy goodnefs ever enlarge her heart: and may that life which thou haſt ſpared, * *and that infant Life which thou haſt given*, be devoted to thy obedience and ſervice, through JESUS CHRIST our LORD. *Amen.*

¶ *Though the foregoing Occaſional Forms are calculated for a confiderable variety of Circumſtances; yet the Miniſter is at liberty to introduce ſuch Forms of his own, as he may more perfectly adapt to the circumſtances of the time, and his Congregation: and this he may do, either by introducing them in ſome proper part of the Service; or in his Prayer before Sermon; in which the Society hopes to enjoy the peculiar advantages of* FREE PRAYER, *as diſtinguiſhed from the advantages of a* PRECOMPOSED FORM.

THE

* *Only to be read when the Child is living.*

THE
COMMANDMENTS;

¶ *To be read the* First Sunday in every Month, *instead of the* Second Lesson, *in the* EVENING SERVICE, *the Congregation standing.*

GOD spake these words, and said, I AM THE LORD, THY GOD:

THOU shalt have none other gods but me.

THOU shalt not make to thyself any graven image; nor the likeness of any thing which is in heaven above; or in the earth beneath; or in the water under the earth: thou shalt not bow down to them, nor worship them; for I, the LORD, thy GOD, am a jealous GOD; and visit the sins of the Fathers upon

THE COMMANDMENTS.

the Children, unto the third and fourth generation of them who hate me; and shew mercy unto thousands in them who love me, and keep my commandments.

Thou shalt not take the Name of the LORD, thy GOD in vain: for the LORD will not hold him guiltless, who taketh his Name in vain.

Remember that thou keep holy the Sabbath Day: six days shalt thou labour and do all that thou hast to do; but the Seventh Day is the Sabbath of the LORD, thy GOD; in it, thou shalt do no manner of work; thou, and thy son, and thy daughter, thy man-servant, and thy maid-servant, thy cattle, and the stranger that is within thy gates. For in six days the LORD made heaven, and earth, the sea, and all that in them is; and rested the Seventh Day: wherefore the LORD blessed the Seventh Day, and hallowed it.

Honour

THE COMMANDMENTS.

Honour thy Father, and thy Mother; that thy days may be long in the land, which the LORD, thy GOD, giveth thee.

Thou shalt do no Murder.

Thou shalt not commit Adultery.

Thou shalt not Steal.

Thou shalt not bear false Witness against thy Neighbour.

Thou shalt not covet thy Neighbour's House; thou shalt not covet thy Neighbour's Wife; nor his Man-servant; nor his Maid-servant; nor his Ox; nor his Ass; nor any thing that is thy Neighbour's.

" Hear

THE COMMANDMENTS.

" Hear ye alſo the excellent Summary of the Moral Law, as delivered by our Bleſſed Saviour."

Thou shalt love the LORD, thy GOD, with all thy heart, with all thy soul, and with all thy mind, and with all thy strength: This is the Firſt, and Great Commandment: and the Second is like unto it.

Thou shalt love thy Neighbour as thyself: and whatsoever ye would that men should do to you, do ye even so to them.

PSALMS
FOR
DIVINE WORSHIP.

PSALM I. *To GOD the Creator.*

Common Metre.

I.

GREAT firſt of Beings! mighty LORD
  Of all this wond'rous frame!
Produc'd by thy creating word,
  The world from nothing came.

II.

Thy voice ſent forth the high command;
  T'was inſtantly obey'd:
And thro' thy goodneſs all things ſtand,
  Which by thy pow'r were made.

III.

Thy glories ſhine throughout the whole,
  Each part reflects thy light:

B

For thee in courfe the planets roll,
  And day fucceeds the night.

IV.

For thee the fun difperfes heat,
  And beams of cheering day:
The diftant ftars in order fet,
  By night thy pow'r difplay.

V.

For thee the earth its produce yields;
  For thee the waters flow:
And various plants adorn the fields,
  And trees afpiring grow.

VI.

Infpir'd with praife, our minds purfue
  This wife and noble end;
And all we think, and all we do
  Shall to thine honour tend.

Psalm II.

To GOD the Creator and Lord of all.

Common Metre.

I.

ALMIGHTY GOD! thy pow'rful word
  From nothing all things brought:
Earth, feas, and fkies, by thee their LORD,
  With fkill divine were wrought.

II.

By thee preferv'd the world remains
  A proof of pow'r divine:
Whatever this great whole contains,
  By fov'reign right is thine.

III.

Sun, moon and stars thy mind fulfil;
 For thee each planet rolls:
Earth, seas, and skies obey thy will;
 Thy power the world controls.

IV.

Thou over all art LORD supreme,
 All things from thee derive:
No creature can dispute thy claim,
 Or independant live.

V.

To thine all-gracious pow'r we bow,
 Our wills to thee resign:
Accept the praise; accept the vow;
 We wou'd be ever thine.

Psalm III. *To GOD the Creator.*

Common Metre.

I.

LET all the just to GOD with joy,
 Their chearful voices raise;
For well the righteous it becomes,
 To sing glad songs of praise.

II.

By his almighty word at first
 The heavenly arch was rear'd;
And all the beauteous hosts of light
 At his command appear'd.

III.

The swelling floods together roll'd,
 He makes in heaps to lie;

And lays as in a ſtore-houſe ſafe,
   His wat'ry treaſures by.

IV.
Let earth and all that dwell therein,
   Before him rev'rent ſtand;
For when he ſpake the word, t'was made,
   T'was fix'd at his command.

V.
Whate'er the mighty LORD decrees
   Shall ſtand for ever ſure;
The ſettled purpoſe of his heart
   To ages ſhall endure.

VI.
The riches of thy mercy, LORD,
   Do thou to us extend;
Since we for all we want, and wiſh,
   On thee alone depend.

PSALM IV. *To GOD our Creator.*

Long Metre.

I.
SING to the LORD with joyful voice;
   Let every land his name adore;
The *Britiſh* iſles ſhall ſend the noiſe
   A-croſs the ocean to the ſhore.

II.
Nations, attend before his throne
   With ſolemn fear, with chearful joy;
Know that the LORD is GOD alone,
   He can create and he deſtroy.

OF PRAISE.

III.
His sov'reign pow'r, without our aid,
   Made us of clay and form'd us men;
And when like wand'ring sheep we stray'd,
   He brought us to his fold again.

IV.
We are his people, we his care,
   Our souls and all our mortal frame;
What lasting honours shall we rear,
   Almighty Maker, to thy name!

V.
We'll croud thy gates with thankful songs;
   High as the heav'ns our voices raise;
And earth with her ten thousand tongues,
   Shall fill thy courts with sounding praise.

VI.
Wide as the world is thy command,
   Vast as eternity thy love:
Firm as a rock thy truth must stand,
   When rolling years shall cease to move.

PSALM V. *To GOD our Creator.*

Long Metre.

I.
WITH one consent let all the earth
   To GOD their chearful voices raise;
Glad homage pay with awful mirth,
   And sing before him songs of praise.

II.
Convinc'd that he is GOD alone,
   From whom both we and all proceed;

We whom he chufes for his own,
　The flock whom he vouchfafes to feed.

III.

O enter then his temple gate!
　Thence to his courts devoutly prefs;
And ftill your grateful hymns repeat,
　And ftill his name with praifes blefs.

IV.

For he's the LORD, fupremely good,
　His mercy is for ever fure;
His truth, which always firmly ftood,
　To endlefs ages fhall endure.

PSALM VI. *To GOD the Creator.*

Common Metre.

I.

O LORD, how excellent thy name!
　How glorious to behold;
Engraven fair on all thy works,
　In characters of gold.

II.

On heav'ns unmeafurable face,
　In lines immenfely great;
In fmall, on ev'ry leaf and flow'r,
　Creator GOD is writ.

III.

Tho' reafon be not given to all,
　Nor voice to thee, O fun!
Their maker all proclaim, and here
　Their language is but one.

IV.

From land to land, and world to world,
  Thy fame is echo'd round;
And ages, as they paſs, tranſmit
  The never-dying ſound.

V.

Angels, the eldeſt ſons of light,
  Began the lofty ſong;
They ſaw the heavens expand abroad,
  And earth on nothing hung.

VI.

Then man, the laſt and nobleſt work,
  Of all this nether frame,
With the firſt vital breath he drew
  Confeſt from whence he came.

VI.

O let us all give praiſe to GOD,
  And magnify his name;
His gracious and his mighty works
  To all the world proclaim.

Psalm VII. *To the Creator.*
Proper Metre.
I.

Ye tribes of Adam, join
  With heaven and earth and ſeas,
And offer notes divine
To your Creator's praiſe:
    Ye holy throng
    Of angels bright,
    In worlds of light
    Begin the ſong.

II.

Thou sun with dazzling rays,
And moon who rul'st the night,
Shine to your maker's praise,
With stars of twinkling light:
    His pow'r declare
    Ye floods on high,
    And clouds that fly,
    In empty air.

III.

The shining worlds above,
In glorious order stand,
Or in swift courses move,
By his supreme command:
    He spake the word,
    And all their frame
    From nothing came
    And praise the LORD.

IV.

He mov'd their mighty wheels
In unknown ages past;
And each his word fulfils,
While time and nature last:
    In diff'rent ways
    His works proclaim,
    His wond'rous name,
    And speak his praise.

V.

Let all the nations fear,
The GOD who rules above;
He brings his people near,
And makes them taste his love.

While earth and sky
Attempt his praise;
His saints shall raise
His honours high.

PSALM VIII. *To GOD the Creator.*
Proper Tune.

I.

HAIL voice divine! thus the Almighty said,
"Let there be light, now let a world be made:"
Light and a world there were; obedient rise
Sun, planets, stars, earth, seas, and spreading skies.

II.

Obedient to thy will, this teeming earth
To beasts and worms of every kind gave birth:
With flocks, and herds, the plains were richly stor'd,
And herbs and fruits did proper food afford.

III.

And last, to finish what thou had'st design'd,
(Of clay like theirs, but with a nobler mind)
ADAM was made; made sov'reign of the rest,
And with his Maker's form divine imprest.

IV.

Benignity and skill and power divine
In the great whole, and ev'ry part did shine:
Fair in its Maker's eye creation stood,
He view'd it well, and pleas'd, pronounc'd it good.

V.

May all thy works, O LORD, resound thy name,
Applaud thy skill; thy pow'r, and love proclaim:
But above all below let man exert
The noblest passions of his grateful heart.

C

Psalm IX.

To GOD the Creator of Mankind.

Common Metre.

I.

GOD of our lives, whose bounteous care
   First gave us pow'r to move;
How shall our thankful hearts declare
   The wonders of thy love.

II.

While void of thought and sense we lay,
   Dust of our parent earth;
Thy breath inform'd the sleeping clay
   And call'd us into birth.

III.

From thee our limbs their fashion took,
   And e'er our life began;
Within the volume of thy book,
   Were written ev'ry one.

IV.

Thine eye beheld in perfect view
   The yet unfinish'd plan;
Th' imperfect lines thy pencil drew,
   And form'd the future man.

V.

O may this frame, which rising grew
   Beneath thy forming hands;
Be studious ever to pursue,
   Whate'er thy will commands.

Of PRAISE.

Psalm X.

To GOD the Creator of Mankind.

Long Metre.

I.

TWAS from thy hand, my GOD, I came,
A work of such a curious frame:
In me thy various wonders shine,
And each proclaims thy skill divine.

II.

Thine eyes did all my limbs survey,
Which yet in dark confusion lay:
Thou saw'st the daily growth they took,
Form'd by the model of thy book.

III.

By thee my growing parts were nam'd;
And what thy sov'reign counsels fram'd,
(The breathing lungs, the beating heart,)
Was copy'd with unerring art.

IV.

At last to show my Maker's name,
He stamp'd his image on my frame;
And in some unknown minute join'd
The finish'd members to a mind.

V.

There the young seeds of thought began,
And all the passions of the man:
Great GOD, our wond'rous nature pays
Immortal tribute to thy praise.

Psalm XI.

The Wisdom of GOD in the formation of Man.

Common Metre.

I.
WHEN I with pleasing wonder stand
  And all my frame survey,
LORD, 'tis thy work; I own the hand
  That built my humble clay.

II.
Thy hand my heart and reins possest,
  Where unborn nature grew:
Thy wisdom all my features trac'd,
  And all my members drew.

III.
Thine eye with nicest care survey'd,
  The growth of ev'ry part;
Till the whole scheme thy thoughts had laid,
  Was copy'd by thy art.

IV.
Heav'n, earth, and sea, and fire and wind
  Declare thy wond'rous skill:
But we review ourselves, and find
  Divine wonders still.

V.
Goodness and wisdom round me shine,
  My form proclaims thy praise:
And with my tongue my soul shall join
  To celebrate thy praise.

Psalm XII.

GOD our Father and Friend.

Proper Tune.

I.

THE LORD JEHOVAH reigns,
His throne is built on high;
The garments he assumes
Are light and majesty:
 His glories shine
 With beams so bright,
 No mortal eye
 Can bear the sight.

II.

The thunders of his hand
Keep the wide world in awe;
His truth and justice stand
To guard his holy law:
 And where his love
 Resolves to bless,
 His truth confirms,
 And seals the grace.

III.

And will this gracious king
Of glory condescend?
Will he declare himself,
" My father and my friend;"
 I love his name,
 I love his word;
 Join all my pow'rs,
 And praise the LORD.

Psalm XIII.

Confidence in GOD our Father.

Common Metre.

I.

O GOD, on thee we all depend,
   On thy paternal care:
Thou wilt the father and the friend
   In ev'ry act appear.

II.

With open hand and lib'ral heart,
   Thou wilt our wants supply:
Thy heav'nly blessings still impart,
   And no good thing deny.

III.

Our father knows what's good and fit,
   And wisdom guides his love:
To thine appointments we submit,
   And ev'ry choice approve.

IV.

In thy paternal love and care,
   With chearful heart we trust;
Thy tender mercies boundless are,
   And all thy thoughts are just.

V.

We cannot want while GOD provides,
   What he allots is best:
And heav'n, whate'er we want besides,
   Will give eternal rest:

PSALM XIV. *To GOD the Preserver.*

Long Metre.

I.

THE earth, and all the heav'nly frame,
   Their great Creator's love proclaim:
He gives the sun his genial pow'r,
   And sends the soft refreshing show'r.

II.

The ground with plenty blooms again,
   And yeilds her various fruits to men:
To men, who from thy bounteous hand,
   Receive the gifts of every land.

III.

Nor to the human race alone,
   Is his paternal goodness shown;
The tribes of earth and sea and air
   Enjoy his universal care.

IV.

Not ev'n a sparrow yeilds it's breath,
   Till GOD permits the stroke of death:
He hears the ravens when they call,
   The father, and the friend of all.

PSALM XV. *To GOD our Preserver.*

Common Metre.

I.

GREAT GOD! to thee, our grateful tongues,
   United thanks shall raise:
Inspire our hearts to tune the songs,
   Which celebrate thy praise,

II.

From thine almighty forming hand,
  We drew our vital pow'rs:
Our time revolves at thy command
  In all it's circling hours.

III.

Thy pow'r, our ever-prefent guard,
  From ev'ry ill defends:
While num'rous dangers hover round,
Onr help from thee defcends.

IV.

Beneath the fhadow of thy wings
  How fweet is our repofe:
The morning light renews the fprings,
  From whence our comfort flows.

V.

In celebration of thy praife,
  We would employ our breath:
And walking fteadfaft in thy ways,
  Will triumph e'en in death.

PSALM XVI.

GOD our Shepherd and Guardian.

Long Metre.

I.

AS the good fhepherd gently leads,
  His wand'ring flocks to verdant meads,
Where peaceful rivers foft and flow,
Amidft the pleafing landfcapes flow:

II.

So GOD, the guardian of our souls,
Our wand'ring foot-steps all controls:
When loft in sins perplexing maze,
He leads us back to wisdom's ways.

III.

Tho' we muſt journey through the plains,
Where death with all it's horror reigns;
Our ſteadfaſt heart no ill ſhall fear,
For thou, O LORD, art with us there.

IV.

By thee with peace and plenty bleſt,
Our lives are one perpetual feaſt:
Thine ever-watchful providence
Is our ſupport and our defence.

V.

O bounteous GOD, our future days
Shall be devoted to thy praiſe;
And in thy houſe, thy ſacred name
And endleſs love ſhall be our theme.

PSALM XVII.   *GOD our Shepherd.*

Long Metre.

I.

OUR ſhepherd is the living LORD;
Now ſhall our wants be well ſupply'd:
His providence and holy word
Become our ſafety and our guide.

II.

In paſtures where ſalvation grows,
He makes us feed, he makes us reſt:

There living water gently flows,
And all the food's divinely bleft.
III.
Our wand'ring feet his ways miftake,
But he reftores our fouls to peace;
And leads us for his mercy's fake
In the fair paths of righteoufnefs.
IV.
Tho' we walk thro' the gloomy vale,
Where death and all it's terrors are;
Our heart and hope fhall never fail,
For GOD our fhepherd's with us there.
V.
Amidft the darkeft fcenes of grief
Thou art our comfort, thou our ftay:
Thy ftaff affords a kind relief,
Thy rod directs our doubtful way.
VI.
Surely the mercies of the LORD
Attend his children all their days:
Here will we dwell to hear his word,
To feek his face, and fing his praife.

Psalm XVIII. *GOD our Shepherd.*

Common Metre.

I.

THE LORD himfelf, the mighty LORD
  Vouchfafes to be our guide:
With more than fhepherd's tender care
  Our wants are all fupply'd,

II.

His goodness leads us to the place
  Where heav'nly pasture grows:
Where living waters gently pass,
  And full salvation flows.

III.

Tho' we too often go astray,
  He doth us still restore;
And guides us in his own right way;
  O may we sin no more. !

IV.

While thus our GOD affords his aid,
  We cannot yield to fear :
Tho' we should walk through death's dark shade,
  Our shepherd's with us there.

PSALM XIX. *To GOD our Preserver.*

Long Metre.

I.

TO heaven my grateful soul ascends,
  On GOD alone for help depends:
His presence my continual guard;
His grace the source of my reward.

II.

The spreading skies by power divine,
In all their radiant glories shine:
From his command, the solid earth
And all it's stores, deriv'd their birth.

III.

Inspected by all-piercing eyes,
No threat'ning snares my soul surprise:
My trembling feet he safely keeps;
My faithful shepherd never sleeps.

IV.

My soul, thy keeper is the LORD;
How great his pow'r! how sure his word!
He spreads a shade on my right hand,
And will a safe retreat command.

V.

Protected by his guardian arm,
Should dreadful scenes our souls alarm;
Our lives are safe: his heav'nly care
Defends us still from ev'ry snare.

VI.

He guides our feet, he guards our way;
His morning smiles bless all the day:
By him our mortal lives are blest;
His favour crowns with endless rest.

PSALM XX.

Dependance on GOD and hope in his Goodness.

Common Metre.

I.

MY GOD, my everlasting hope,
   I live upon thy truth:
Thine hands have held my childhood up,
   And strengthn'd all my youth.

II.

My flesh was fashion'd by thy pow'r
  With all these limbs of mine:
And from my mother's painful hour,
  I've been entirely thine.

III.

Still has my life new wonders seen
  With each returning year:
Behold my days which yet remain,
  I trust them to thy care.

IV.

Cast me not off when strength declines,
  When hoary hairs arise:
And round me let thy goodness shine,
  When e'er thy servant dies.

V.

Then in the hist'ry of my age,
  When men review my days;
They'll read thy love in ev'ry page,
  In ev'ry line thy praise.

Psalm XXI.

GOD our all-sufficient dependance.

As the 113 Psalm.

I.

O HAPPY nation, where the LORD
  Reveals the treasure of his word,
    And builds his church, his earthly throne.
His eye the heathen world surveys,
He form'd their hearts, he knows their ways,
    But GOD their maker is unknown.

II.

Let kings rely upon their hoft;
And of his ftrength the champion boaft;
   In vain they boaft, in vain rely:
In vain we truft the brutal force,
The fpeed or courage of a horfe,
   To guard his rider, or to fly.

III.

Thy providence, almighty LORD,
Doth more fecure defence afford
   When death, or dangers threat'ning ftand.
Thy watchful eye preferves the juft,
Who make thy name their fear and truft,
   When wars, or famine wafte the land.

IV.

In ficknefs, or the bloody field,
Thou our phyfician, thou our fhield;
   Send us falvation from thy throne:
We wait to fee thy goodnefs fhine;
Let us rejoice in help divine;
   O GOD, in thee we hope alone.

Psalm XXII.

Prefervation of Life from GOD.

Common Metre.

I.

LORD, unto thee we lift our eyes,
   On thee our hopes are laid:
Thou who didft build the earth and fkies,
   Art our fufficient aid:

II.

GOD guides our feet, and guards our way,
    With an almighty arm:
Preserves us safe, both night and day,
    From all destructive harm.

III.

What tho' thy providence should call
    Where death displays it's pow'r;
Short of our lives the shafts shall fall,
    Till GOD appoints the hour.

Psalm XXIII.

GOD's Defence our Security.

As the 113th Psalm.

I.

HE who has GOD his guardian made
    Shall under his almighty shade
    Secure and undisturb'd abide:
This man with joy divine may say,
He is my fortress and my stay;
    Who always hath my wants supply'd.

II.

For all whose well-plac'd confidence
Have made the LORD their sure defence,
    May rest upon his promises:
Either no ill shall them o'ertake;
Or else their very suff'rings make
    Their hearts and lives prepar'd for bliss.

Psalm XXIV.

GOD the Preserver to be adored.

Common Metre.

I.

THY works of glory, mighty LORD,
　　Thy wonders in the deeps,
The sons of courage shall record,
　　Who trade in floating ships.

II.

At thy command the winds arise,
　　And swell the tow'ring waves:
The men astonish'd mount the skies,
　　And sink in op'ning graves.

III.

Then to the LORD they raise their cries;
　　He hears the loud request;
And orders silence thro' the skies,
　　And lays the floods to rest.

IV.

Sailors rejoice to lose their fears,
　　And see the storm allay'd:
Now to their eyes the port appears,
　　There let their vows be paid.

V.

'Tis GOD that brings them safe to land;
　　Let thoughtless mortals know,
That waves are under his command,
　　And all the winds that blow.

VI.

O that the sons of men would praise
  The goodness of the LORD!
And those who see thy wond'rous ways,
  Thy wond'rous love record.

Psalm XXV.

Preserving Goodness acknowledged.

Common Metre.

I.

How are thy servants blest, O LORD!
  How sure is their defence!
Eternal wisdom is their guide,
  Their help omnipotence.

II.

In foreign realms, and lands remote,
  Supported by thy care;
Through burning climes I pass'd unhurt,
  And breath'd in tainted air.

III.

Thy mercy sweeten'd ev'ry soil,
  Made ev'ry region please;
The hoary frozen hills it warm'd,
  And smooth'd the boist'rous seas.

IV.

Think, O my soul, devoutly think,
  How with affrighted eyes,
Thou saw'st the wide extended deep,
  In all its horrors rise!

V.

Confusion dwelt in ev'ry face,
  And fear in ev'ry heart;
When waves on waves, and gulphs on gulphs,
  O'ercame the pilot's art.

VI.

Yet then from all my griefs, O LORD,
  Thy mercy set me free;
Whilst in the confidence of pray'r
  My soul took hold on thee.

VII.

For though in dreadful whirles we hung,
  High on the broken wave;
I knew thou wer't not slow to hear,
  Nor impotent to save.

VIII.

The storm was laid, the winds retir'd,
  Obedient to thy will:
The sea that roar'd at thy command,
  At thy command was still.

IX.

In midst of dangers, fears, and death,
  Thy goodness I'll adore;
And praise thee for thy mercies past,
  And humbly hope for more.

X.

My life, whilst thou preserv'st my life,
  Thy sacrifice shall be;
And death, when death shall be my doom,
  Shall join my soul to thee.

Psalm XXVI.

To the ONE GOD.

Long Metre.

I.

ETERNAL GOD, almighty caufe
Of earth, and feas, and worlds unknown:
The world fubmits to all thy laws,
Depends entire on thee alone.

II.

Thy gorious being fingly ftands,
Of all within it felf poffeft:
Controul'd by none are thy commands;
And in thy felf completely bleft.

III.

To thee alone ourfelves we owe;
Let heav'n and earth the homage pay:
All other Gods we difavow,
Deny their claims, renounce their fway.

IV.

In thee alone we feek for blifs,
Thou great original of love;
There all our wealth and treafure is;
The world would infufficient prove.

V.

Spread thy great name thro' *Gentile* lands,
Their idol deities dethrone:
Reduce the world to thy command,
And reign, as thou art GOD, alone.

Psalm XXVII. *GOD Eternal.*

Common Metre.

I.

RISE, rife, my foul, and leave the groun,
    Stretch all thy thoughts abroad:
And raife up ev'ry tuneful found,
    To praife the eternal GOD.

II.

His boundlefs years can ne'er decreafe,
    But ftill maintain their prime:
ETERNITY's his dwelling place,
    And EVER is his time.

III.

Whilft like a tide our minutes flow,
    The prefent and the paft;
He fills his own immortal NOW,
    And fees our ages wafte.

IV.

The feas and fkies muft perifh too,
    And vaft deftruction come:
And all things as they older grow,
    Approach their final doom.

V.

But tho' the fea fhrink all away,
    And flames melt down the fkies;
Our GOD fhall live in endlefs day,
    When this creation dies.

Psalm XXVIII.

GOD's eternal Dominion.

Common Metre.

I.

GREAT GOD! how infinite art thou!
   Imperfect mortals we!
Let the whole race of creatures bow,
   And give their praise to thee.

II.

Thy throne eternal ages stood,
   E'er earth or heavens were made;
Thou art the ever living GOD,
   Were all the nations dead.

III.

Nature and time unveiled lie
   To thine immense survey;
From the formation of the sky,
   To the great final day.

IV.

Our lives thro' various scenes are drawn,
   And vex'd with trifling cares:
But thine eternal thought moves on
   Thine undisturb'd affairs.

V.

Great GOD! how infinite art thou!
   Imperfect mortals we!
Let the whole race of creatures bow!
   And pay their praise to thee.

Psalm XXIX.

GOD eternal, and Man mortal.

Common Metre.

I.

O GOD our help in ages paſt,
  Our hope for years to come!
Our ſhelter from the ſtromy blaſt,
  And our eternal home.

II.

Before the hills in order ſtood,
  Or earth receiv'd her frame!
From everlaſting thou art GOD,
  To endleſs years the ſame.

III.

Thy word commands our fleſh to duſt,
  "Return ye ſons of men"
All nations roſe from earth at firſt,
  And turn to earth again,

IV.

Time like an overflowing ſtream
  Bears all its ſons away:
They fly, forgotten, as a dream
  Dies at the op'ning day.

V.

O GOD our help in ages paſt,
  Our hope for days to come,
Our ſhelter from the ſtormy blaſt,
  And our eternal home.

PSALM XXX. *GOD Omnipresent.*

Common Metre.

I.

IN all my vast concerns with thee,
   In vain my soul wou'd try,
To shun thy presence, LORD, or flee
   The notice of thine eye.

II.

Thine all-surrounding sight surveys
   My rising and my rest;
My public walks, my private ways,
   And secrets of my breast.

III.

My thoughts lie open to the Lord
   Before they're form'd within;
And e're my lips pronounce the word,
   He knows the sense I mean.

IV.

O wond'rous knowledge, deep and high!
   Where can a creature hide?
Within thy circling arms I lie,
   Beset on every side.

V.

If wing'd with beams of morning-light
   I fly beyond the west,
Thy hands, which must support my flight,
   Would soon betray my rest.

VI.

If o'er my sins I think to draw,
   The curtains of the night,

Those flaming eyes that guard thy law
  Wou'd turn the shades to light.

VII.

The beams of noon, the midnight-hour,
  Are both alike to thee;
O may I ne'er provoke that pow'r,
  From which I cannot flee!

PSALM XXXI. *The All-seeing GOD.*

Long Metre.

I.

LORD, thou hast search'd and seen me thro';
Thine eye commands with piercing view
My rising and my resting hours;
My heart and flesh with all their powers.

II.

My thoughts, before they are my own,
Are to my GOD distinctly known:
He knows the words I mean to speak,
E'er from my op'ning lips they break.

III.

Within thy circling power I stand;
On every side I find thy hand:
Awake, asleep, at home, abroad,
I am surrounded still with GOD.

IV.

Amazing knowledge, vast and great!
What large extent! what lofty height!
My soul with all the pow'rs I boast,
Is in the boundless prospect lost.

V.

O may these thoughts possess my breast,
Where-e'er I rove, where-e'er I rest!
Nor let my weaker passions dare
Consent to sin, for GOD is there.

Pause I.

VI.

Could I so false, so faithless prove,
To quit thy service and thy love,
Where, LORD, could I thy presence shun,
Or from thy dreadful glory run?

VII.

If up to heaven I take my flight,
'Tis there thou dwell'st enthron'd in light;
Or dive to hell, there vengeance reigns,
And *Satan* groans beneath thy chains.

VIII.

If mounted on a morning-ray
I fly beyond the *western* sea,
Thy swifter hand would first arrive,
And there arrest thy fugitive.

IX.

Or should I try to shun thy sight
Beneath the spreading veil of night,
One glance of thine, one piercing ray,
Wou'd kindle darkness into day.

X.

O may these thoughts possess my breast,
Where-e'er I rove, where-e'er I rest!
Nor let my weaker passions dare
Consent to sin, for GOD is there.

Pause II.

XI.
The veil of night is no difguife,
No fcreen from thy all-fearching eyes;
Thy hand can feize thy foes as foon
Thro' midnight-fhades as blazing noon.

XII.
Midnight and noon in this agree,
Great GOD, they're both alike to thee;
No death can hide what GOD will fpy,
And hell lies naked to his eye.

XIII.
O may thefe thoughts poffefs my breaft,
Where-e'er I rove, where-e'er I reft!
Nor let my weaker paffions dare
Confent to fin, for GOD is there.

Psalm XXXII.

The Power of GOD.

Common Metre.

I.
'TWAS GOD who fix'd the rolling fpheres,
   And ftretch'd the boundlefs fkies;
Who form'd the plan of endlefs years,
   And bade the ages rife.

II.
From everlafting is his might;
   Immenfe and unconfin'd:
He pierces thro' the realms of light,
   And rides upon the wind.

III.

He darts along the burning skies,
  Loud thunders round him roar:
All heaven attends him as he flies,
  All hell proclaims his power.

IV.

He speaks; great nature's wheels stand still,
  And leave their wonted round:
The mountains melt; each trembling hill
  Forsakes its antient bound.

V.

He scatters nations with his breath;
  The scatter'd nations fly:
Blue pestilence, and spreading death
  Confess the godhead nigh.

VI.

Ye worlds, and every living thing,
  Fulfil his high command;
Pay duteous homage to your King
  And own his ruling hand.

PSALM XXXIII.

The Power of GOD.

Long Metre.

I.

O COME loud anthems let us sing,
  Loud thanks to our almighty king;
High let us raise our grateful voice,
When in JEHOVAH we rejoice.

II.

The LORD, our GOD, inthron'd in state,
Is with unrivall'd glory great;
A King superior far to all,
Whom Gods the heathen falsely call.

III.

The depths of earth are in his hand,
Her secret stores at his command:
The strength of hills which threat the skies,
Subject to his great empire lies.

IV.

The rolling ocean's vast abyss,
By the same sov'reign right is his;
'Tis mov'd by his almighty hand,
Who form'd and fix'd the solid land.

V.

In thee the sov'reign right remains
Of all that earth or heaven contains;
Angels and men thee LORD alone,
King, maker, and preserver own.

VI.

Thine arm is mighty, strong thy hand,
Possess'd of absolute command:
Yet, LORD, thou dost with justice reign,
And truth and mercy still maintain.

PSALM XXXIV.

The Majesty and Power of GOD.

Long Metre.

I.

YE sons of men, in sacred lays
Attempt your great Creator's praise;

But O what tongue can speak his fame;
What mortal verse can reach the theme!

II.

Enthron'd amidst the radiant spheres,
He glory like a garment wears:
And boundless wisdom, power, and grace,
Command our awe, invite our praise.

III.

To GOD all nature owes its birth,
He form'd this pond'rous globe of earth;
He rais'd the glorious arch on high,
And measur'd out the azure sky.

IV.

In all our maker's vast designs,
Omnipotence with wisdom shines:
His works thro' all this wond'rous frame,
Bare the great impress of his name.

V.

Rais'd on devotions lofty wing,
Our souls his high perfections sing;
O let his praise employ our tongues,
And list'ning worlds approve the songs.

Psalm XXXV.

The Power and Majesty of GOD.
Common Metre.

I.

WITH rev'rence let the saints appear,
 And bow before the LORD;
His high commands with rev'rence hear,
And listen to his word.

II.

How wonderful thy glories are!
  How bright thine armies shine!
Thy pow'r is great beyond compare,
  No truth so firm as thine.

III.

The northern pole, and southern rest
  On thy supporting hand:
Darkness and day, from east to west,
  Move round at thy command.

IV.

Thy words the raging winds controul,
  And rule the boist'rous deep:
Thou mak'st the sleeping billows roll,
  The rolling billows sleep.

V.

Heav'n, earth, and air, and sea are thine,
  And the dark world of hell:
How can thine arm in vengeance shine
  When mortals dare rebel!

IV.

Justice and judgment are thy throne;
  Yet wond'rous is thy grace:
And truth and mercy join'd in one,
  Invite us near thy face.

OF PRAISE.

PSALM XXXVI.
The Power of GOD in his Works.
Proper Metre.

I.

ARISE my soul, on wings devout arise,
To praise th' almighty sov'reign of the skies;
In whom alone unspotted glory shines,
Which not the heav'ns, nor boundless space confines.

II.

He spread the firmament from pole to pole;
And hea'venly light diffus'd throughout the whole:
Of liquid air he bad the columns rise,
Which prop the starry concave of the skies.

III.

His word in air this pond'rous earth sustain'd,
"Be fixt," he said —— and fixt the earth remain'd:
Heav'n, air and sea, tho' all their storms combine,
Shake not its base, nor break the law divine.

IV.

He bade the changing moon adorn the night,
Revolve her circle and increase her light:
Assign'd a province to each rolling sphere,
And taught the sun to regulate the year.

V.

Thou from the realms of everlasting day,
See'st all thy works at one immense survey;
Pleas'd at one view the whole to comprehend,
Part joind to part, concurring to one end.

VI.

Hail sov'reign goodness! all creating mind!
On all thy works thyself inscrib'd we find:
How various all, how variously indu'd!
How great their number, and each part how good!

Psalm XXXVII.

The Greatness and Majesty of GOD.

As the 113 Psalm.

I.

YE holy souls in GOD rejoice,
  Your maker's praise becomes your voice;
  Great is your theme, your songs be new;
Sing of his name, his works and ways,
His works of nature and of grace,
  How wise and holy, just and true!

II.

Justice and truth he ever loves,
And the whole earth his goodness proves;
  His word the heavenly arches spread;
Far as they shine from north to south:
And by the spirit of his mouth,
  Were all the shining armies made.

III.

He gathers the wide flowing seas;
Those wat'ry treasures know their place,
  In the vast store-house of the deep;
He spake and gave all nature birth;
And fires, and seas, and heaven and earth,
  His everlasting orders keep.

IV.

Mortals be humble, and adore
A GOD of such resistless pow'r;
  Nor dare indulge your feeble rage,
Vain are your thoughts and weak your hands:
But his eternal counsel stands,
  And rules the world from age to age.

Psalm XXXVIII.
GOD's universal Dominion.
Short Metre.

I.
THE LORD, the sov'reign king,
 Hath fix'd his throne on high;
O'er all the heav'nly world he rules,
 And all beneath the sky.

II.
Ye angels, great in might,
 And swift to do his will,
Bless ye, the LORD, whose voice ye hear,
 Whose pleasure ye fulfil.

III.
Let the bright hosts, who wait
 The orders of their king,
And guard his churches when they pray,
 Join in the praise they sing.

IV.
While all his wond'rous works,
 Thro' his vast kingdoms show
Their Maker's glory, thou my soul
 Shalt sing his praises too.

Psalm XXXIX.
The eternal and sovereign GOD.
Long Metre.

I.
JEHOVAH reigns: he dwells in light,
 Girded with majesty and might:
The world, created by his hands,
Still on its first foundation stands.

II.

But e'er this spacious world was made,
Or had its first foundations laid,
Thy throne eternal ages stood,
Thyself the ever-living GOD.

III.

Like floods the angry nations rise,
And aim their rage againſt the ſkies;
Vain floods that aim their rage ſo high!
At thy rebuke the billows die.

IV.

For ever ſhall thy throne endure;
Thy promiſe ſtands for ever ſure;
And everlaſting holineſs
Becomes the dwellings of thy grace.

Psalm XL.

The Majeſty and Condeſcenſion of GOD.

As the 113th Psalm.

I.

YE that delight to ſerve the LORD,
  The honours of his name record,
His ſacred name for ever bleſs:
Where-e'er the circling ſun diſplays
His riſing beams, or ſetting rays,
  Let lands and ſeas his pow'r confeſs.

II.

Not time, nor nature's narrow rounds,
Can give his vaſt dominion bounds;
  The heav'ns are far below his height:

OF PRAISE.

Let no created greatness dare
With our eternal GOD compare,
  Arm'd with his uncreated might.

III.

He bows his glorious head to view
What the bright hosts of angels do,
  And bends his care to mortal things;
His sov'reign hand exalts the poor,
He takes the needy from the door,
  And makes them company for kings,

PSALM XLI.

GOD the universal Sovereign.

As the 113th PSALM.

I.

LET all the earth their voices raise
To sing the choicest psalm of praise,
  To sing and bless JEHOVAH's name:
His glory let the heathens know,
His wonders to the nations show,
  And all his saving works proclaim.

II.

The heathens know thy glory, LORD;
The wond'ring nations read thy word,
  In *Britain* is JEHOVAH known:
Our worship shall no more be paid
To Gods which mortal hands have made;
  Our Maker is our GOD alone.

III.

He fram'd the globe, he built the sky,
He made the shining worlds on high,
   And reigns compleat in glory there:
His beams are majesty and light;
His beauties how divinely bright!
   His temple how divinely fair!

IV.

Come the great day, the glorious hour,
When earth shall feel his saving pow'r,
   And barb'rous nations fear his name:
Then shall the race of men confess
The beauty of his holiness,
   And in his courts his grace proclaim.

PSALM XLII.

The Wisdom of GOD in his Works.

Common Metre.

I.

SONGS of immortal praise belong,
   To our almighty GOD;
He has our heart, and he our tongue,
   To spread his name abroad.

II.

How great the works his hand has wrought!
   How glorious in our sight!
And men in ev'ry age have sought
   His wonders with delight.

III.

How most exact is nature's frame!
   How wise th' eternal mind!

His counsels never change the scheme
  That his first thoughts design'd.
IV.
When he redeem'd his chosen sons,
  He fix'd his cov'nant sure:
The orders that his lips pronounce
  To endless years endure.
V.
Nature and time, and earth and skies;
  Thy heav'nly skill proclaim:
What shall we do to make us wise,
  But learn to read thy name?
VI.
To fear thy pow'r, to trust thy grace,
  Is our divinest skill;
And he's the wisest of our race
  That best obeys thy will.

Psalm XLIII.

The Wisdom of GOD in his Works.

As the 113 Psalm.

I.
GREAT GOD, the heav'ns well order'd frame
Declares the glories of thy name;
  There thy rich works of wonder shine:
A thousand starry beauties there,
A thousand radiant marks appear
  Of boundless pow'r and skill divine.
II.
From night to day, from day to night
The dawning and the dying light

Lectures of heavenly wifdom read:
With filent eloquence they raife
Our thoughts to the Creator's praife,
 And neither found or language need.

III.

Yet their divine inftructions run
Far as the journeys of the fun,
 And every nation knows their voice:
While he, like fome young bridegroom dreft,
Breaks from the chambers of the eaft,
 Shines round, and makes the earth rejoice.

Psalm XLIV.

The divine Goodnefs.

Common Metre.

I.

WHEN all thy mercies, O our GOD,
 Our rifing foul furveys,
Tranfported with the view, we're loft
 In wonder, love and praife.

II.

Thy providence our lives fuftain'd,
 And all our wants redreft,
When in the filent womb we lay,
 Or hung upon the breaft.

IV.

To all our weak complaints and cries
 Thy mercy lent an ear;
E'er yet our feeble thoughts had learnt
 To form themfelves in pray'r.

IV.

Unnumber'd comforts on our fouls
  Thy tender care beftow'd;
Before our infant hearts conceiv'd
  From whence thofe comforts flow'd.

V.

When in the flipp'ry paths of youth,
  With heedlefs fteps we ran,
Thine arm unfeen convey'd us fafe,
  And lead us up to man.

VI.

Thro' hidden dangers, toils and death,
  It gently clear'd our way;
And thro' the pleafing fnares of vice,
  More to be fear'd than they.

VII.

O how fhall words, with equal warmth,
  The gratitude declare,
That glows within my ravifh'd heart!
  But thou can'ft read it there.

PAUSE

VIII.

When all thy mercies, oh our GOD,
  Our rifing foul furveys,
Tranfported with the view, we'er loft
  In wonder, love and praife.

IX.

[When worn with ficknefs, oft haft thou
  With health renew'd our face;
And, when in fins and forrow funk,
  Reviv'd our fouls with grace]

X.

Thy bounteous hand with worldly blifs,
　　Hath made our cup run o'er;
And, in a kind and faithful friend,
　　Hath doubled all our ſtore.

XI.

Ten thouſand thouſand precious gifts
　　Our daily thanks employ;
Nor is the leaſt a chearful heart,
　　That taſtes thoſe gifts with joy.

XII.

Through ev'ry period of our lives,
　　Thy goodneſs we'll purſue;
And after death, in diſtant worlds,
　　The glorious theme renew.

XIII.

When nature fails, and day and night
　　Divide thy works no more,
Our ever grateful hearts, O LORD,
　　Thy mercy ſhall adore.

XIV.

Through all eternity to thee,
　　A joyful ſong we'll raiſe;
For oh! eternity's too ſhort,
　　To utter all thy praiſe.

Psalm XLV.

On the divine Goodneſs.

Common Metre.

I.

LORD thou art good: all nature ſhows
　　Thee full, and free, and kind;
'Thy bounty thro' creation flows,

Nor can it be confin'd.

II.

The whole and ev'ry part proclaims
   Thine infinite good will;
It shines in stars, and flows in streams,
   And bursts from ev'ry hill.

III.

It spreads thro' all the spreading main,
   And heavens which spread more wide,
It drops in gentle show'rs of rain,
   And rolls in ev'ry tide.

IV.

Still hath it been diffus'd and free,
   Thro' ages past and gone;
Nor ever can exhausted be,
   But keeps still flowing on.

V.

Still thro' the whole it pours supplies,
   Spreads joy thro' all the parts;
LORD, may such goodness draw our eyes,
   And captivate our hearts.

VI.

High admiration let it raise,
   And kind affections move;
Employ our tongues in hymns of praise,
   And fill our hearts with love.

Psalm XLVI.

The Goodneſs of GOD unchangeable.

Long Metre.

I.

ETERNAL ſource of ev'ry joy!
Well may thy praiſe our lips employ,
While in thy temple we appear;
Thy goodneſs crowns the circling year.

II.

Wide as the earth and planets roll,
Thy hand ſupports and cheers the whole;
By thee the ſun is taught to riſe,
And darkneſs when to veil the ſkies.

III.

The flow'ry ſpring at thy command,
Embalms the air and paints the land;
The ſummer rays with vigour ſhine,
To raiſe the corn, and cheer the vine.

IV.

Seaſons and months, and weeks and days,
Demand ſucceſſive hymns of praiſe:
Still be the chearful homage paid,
With op'ning light, and ev'ning ſhade.

V.

O may our more harmonious tongues
In worlds unknown purſue the ſongs:
And in thoſe brighter courts adore,
Where days and years revolve no more.

Psalm XLVII.

The Divine Bounty.

Common Metre.

I.

'TIS by thy strength the mountains stand,
  GOD of eternal pow'r,
The sea grows calm at thy command,
  And tempests cease to roar.

II.

The morning light and ev'ning shade
  Successive comforts bring;
Thy plenteous fruits make harvest glad;
  Thy flowers adorn the spring.

III.

Seasons, and times, and months and hours,
  Heav'n, earth and air are thine;
When clouds distil in fruitful show'rs,
  The author is divine.

IV.

Those floating cisterns in the sky
  Borne by the winds around,
With wat'ry treasures well supply,
  The furrows of the ground.

V.

The thirsty ridges drink their fill,
  The ranks of corn appear;
Thy ways abound with blessings still,
  Thy goodness crowns the year.

Psalm XLVIII.

The Goodnefs of GOD.

Common Metre.

I.

SWEET is the mem'ry of thy grace,
  O GOD, our heav'nly king;
Let age to age thy righteoufnefs
  In founds of glory fing.

II.

GOD reigns on high, but not confines
  His goodnefs to the fkies;
Thro' the whole earth his bounty fhines,
  And ev'ry want fupplies.

III.

With longing eyes thy creatures wait,
  On thee for daily food;
Thy lib'ral hand provides their meat,
  And fills their mouths with good.

IV.

How kind are thy compaffions, LORD!
  How flow thine anger moves!
But foon he fends his pardoning word
  To chear the fouls he loves.

V.

Creatures with all their endlefs race
  Thy pow'r and praife proclaim;
But faints that tafte thy richer grace
  Delight to blefs thy name.

Psalm XLIX.

The Goodness of GOD.

Common Metre.

I.

LET ev'ry tongue thy goodness speak,
  Thou sov'reign LORD of all;
Thy strengthning hands uphold the weak,
  And raise the poor that fall.

II.

When sorrow bows the spirit down,
  Or virtue lies distrest
Beneath some proud oppressor's frown,
  Thou giv'st the mourners rest.

III.

The LORD supports our tott'ring days,
  And guides our giddy youth:
Holy and just are all his ways,
  And all his words are truth.

IV.

He know the pain his servants feel,
  He hears his children cry,
And their best wishes to fulfil
  His grace is ever nigh.

V.

His mercy never shall remove
  From men of heart sincere;
He saves the souls, whose humble love
  Is join'd with holy fear.

Psalm L.

The Divine Mercy.

Long Metre.

I.

MY ſoul inſpir'd with ſacred love,
GOD's holy name for ever bleſs,
Of all his favours mindful prove,
And ſtill thy grateful thanks expreſs.

II.

'Tis he who all thy ſins forgives,
And after ſickneſs makes thee ſound;
From danger he thy life retrieves,
By him with grace and mercy crown'd.

III.

The LORD abounds with tender love,
And unexampled acts of grace;
His waken'd wrath doth ſlowly move,
His willing mercy flies apace.

IV.

As high as heav'n its arch extends,
Above this little ſpot of clay;
So much his boundleſs grace tranſcends
The beſt obedience we can pay.

V.

Let ev'ry creature join and bleſs
The mighty LORD: and thou my heart,
With grateful joy thy ſongs expreſs,
And in this conſort bear thy part.

PSALM LI. *Divine Mercy.*
Short Metre.

I.

O BLESS the LORD our souls,
   Let all within us join,
And aid our tongues to bless his name,
   Whose favours are divine.

II.

O bless the LORD my soul,
   Nor let his mercies lie
Forgotten in unthankfulness,
   And without praises die.

III.

'Tis he forgives our sins;
   'Tis he relieves our pain;
'Tis he that heals our sicknesses;
   And makes us young again.

VI.

He crowns our lives with love;
   When ransom'd from the grave;
He that redeems our souls from death,
   Hath sov'reign pow'r to save.

V.

He fills the poor with good;
   He gives the suff'rers rest:
The LORD hath judgments for the proud,
   And justice for th' oppress'd.

VI.

His wond'rous works and ways,
   He made by Moses known:
But sent the world his truth and grace
   By his beloved son.

Psalm LII. *Divine Mercy.*

Short Metre.

I.

OUR souls, repeat his praise
  Whose mercies are so great;
Whose anger is so slow to rise,
  So ready to abate.

II.

GOD will not always chide;
  And when his strokes are felt,
His Strokes are fewer than our crimes,
  And lighter than our guilt.

III.

High as the heav'ns are rais'd
  Above the ground we tread,
So far the riches of his grace
  Our highest thoughts exceed.

IV.

His pow'r subdues our sins,
  And his forgiving love,
Far as the *east* is from the *west*,
  Doth all our guilt remove.

V.

The pity of the LORD
  To those that fear his name,
Is such as tender parents feel;
  He knows our feeble frame.

VI.

He knows we are but dust,
  Scatter'd with ev'ry breath;

His anger like a rising wind
  Can send us swift to death.

VII.
Our days are as the grass,
  Or like the morning-flow'r;
If one sharp blast sweeps o'er the field,
  It withers in an hour.

VIII.
But thy compassions, LORD,
  To endless years endure;
And childrens children ever find
  Thy words of promise sure.

PSALM LIII. *Divine Providence.*

Long Metre.

I.
THRO' all the various shifting scene
  Of life's mistaken ill or good;
Thy hand, O GOD, conducts unseen,
The beautiful vicissitude.

II.
Thou portion'st with paternal care,
How e'er unjustly we complain,
To each their necessary share
Of joy and sorrow, health and pain.

III.
All things on earth, and all in heav'n
On thine eternal will depend;
And all for greater good were given,
Would man pursue th' appointed end.

IV.

Be this our care——to all beside
Indiff'rent let our wishes be:
Passion be calm, and dumb be pride,
And fix'd our souls O GOD on thee.

PSALM LIV.

The Perfections and Providence of GOD

Long Metre.

I.

HIGH in the Heav'ns, eternal GOD,
Thy goodness in full glory shines;
Thy truth shall break thro' ev'ry cloud,
Which veils and darkens thy designs.

II.

For ever firm thy justice stands,
As mountains their foundations keep;
Wise are the wonders of thy hands,
Thy judgments are a mighty deep.

III.

Thy providence is kind and large;
Both man and beast thy bounty share;
The whole creation is thy charge;
The good are thy peculiar care.

IV.

O GOD, how excellent thy grace,
Whence all our hope and comfort springs;
The sons of Adam in distress
Fly to the shadow of thy wings.

Psalm LV.

Dependence upon Providence.

Long Metre.

I.

GREAT LORD of earth, and seas. and [skies,
Thy wealth the needy world supplies:
On thee alone the whole depends,
Thy care to ev'ry part extends.

II.
To thee perpetual thanks we owe,
For all our comforts here below;
Our daily bread thy bounty gives,
And ev'ry rising want relieves.

III.
The wastes of life thy pow'r repairs,
Thy mercy stills tempestuous cares:
And safe beneath thy guardian arm,
We live secur'd from ev'ry harm.

IV.
To thee we chearful homage bring;
In grateful hymns thy praises sing;
Direct to thee our waiting eyes,
And humbly look for fresh supplies.

V.
We still are indigent and poor,
Indebted much, yet lacking more:
On thee we ever will depend,
The rich, the sure, the faithful friend.

VI.

And should thy measures seem severe,
Calmly may we thy chast'ning bear;
Without complaint to thee submit,
Th' unerring judge of what is fit.

Psalm LVI.

Dependence on Providence.

Long Metre.

I.

ON thee, O GOD! we still depend,
  Our father, and our constant friend;
All that is good thou can'st supply,
And put all threat'ning evil by.

II.

Should wars on ev'ry side invade,
We'll shelter seek beneath thy shade:
We'll trust to thy paternal care,
Nor want, nor harm, nor danger fear.

III.

We'll still refer ourselves to thee,
And with our lot contented be;
With one consenting heart and voice,
Approve our heav'nly father's choice.

IV.

From earth we'll turn our longing eyes,
To regions far beyond the skies;
O fit us for that blest abode,
Where dwells our Saviour and our GOD.

OF PRAISE.

PSALM LVII.

Submission to Providence.

Common Metre.

I.

NAKED as from the earth we came,
And crept to life at first,
We to the earth return again,
And mingle with our dust.

II.

The fond delights we here enjoy,
And call our own in vain,
Are but short favours borrow'd now,
To be repaid again.

III.

'Tis GOD that lifts our comforts high,
Or sinks them to the grave;
He gives, and blessed be his name,
He takes but what he gave.

IV.

Peace, all our hasty passions then,
Let each impatient sigh,
Be silent at his sov'reign will,
And ev'ry murmur die.

V.

If smiling mercy crown our lives,
It's praises shall be spread;
And we'll adore the justice too,
That strikes our comforts dead.

Psalm LVIII. *Praise to GOD.*

Short Metre.

I.

ALMIGHTY maker GOD!
 How wond'rous is thy name!
Thy glories how diffus'd abroad
 Thro' all creation's frame.

II.

Nature in ev'ry dress
 Her humble homage pays;
And does a thousand ways express
 Her undissembled praise.

III.

Our souls would rise and sing,
 Our great creator too;
Fain would our tongue adore our king
 And yield the worship due.

IV.

Let joy and worship spend
 The remnant of our days;
And oft to GOD our souls ascend
 In humble acts of praise.

Psalm LIX.

A Song of Praise.

Common Metre.

I.

IN GOD's own house pronounce his praise,
 His grace he there reveals;

To heav'n your joy and wonder raise,
 For there his glory dwells.

II.
Let all your sacred passions move,
 While you rehearse his deeds;
But the great work of saving love,
 Your highest praise exceeds.

III.
All that have motion, life and breath,
 Proclaim your maker blest;
Yet when our voice expires in death,
 Our souls shall praise him best.

Psalm LX.

General Act of Praise.

Long Metre.

I.
BE thou exalted, O my GOD,
 Above the heav'ns where angels dwell;
Thy pow'r on earth be known abroad,
And land to land thy wonders tell.

II.
My heart is fix'd; my tongue shall raise
Immortal honours to thy name;
Awake, my tongue, to sound his praise,
My tongue, the glory of my frame.

III.
High o'er the earth thy mercy reigns,
And reaches to the utmost sky;
His truth to endless years remains,
When lower worlds dissolve and die.

IV.

Be thou exalted, O my GOD,
Above the heav'ns where angels dwell;
Thy pow'r on earth be known abroad,
And land to land thy wonders tell.

PSALM. LXI.

Praife to GOD from all Creatures.

Proper Metre.

I.

YE boundlefs realms of joy,
 Exalt your maker's fame;
His praife your fong employ
Above the ftarry frame:
  Your voices raife,
  Ye cherubim
  And feraphim,
  To fing his praife.

II.

Thou moon that rul'ft the night,
And fun that guid'ft the day,
Ye glitt'ring ftars of light,
To him your homage pay:
  His praife declare,
  Ye heav'ns above,
  And clouds that move
  In liquid air.

III.

Let them adore the LORD,
And praife his holy name,

By whose almighty word
They all from nothing came:
   And all shall last,
   From changes free:
   His firm decree
   Stands ever fast.
IV.
Let earth her tribute pay;
Praise him, ye dreadful whales,
And fish that thro' the sea
Glide swift with glitt'ring scales:
   Fire, hail, and snow,
   And misty air,
   And winds that, where
   He bids them, blow.
V.
By hills and mountains (all
In grateful consort join'd),
By cedars stately tall,
And trees for fruit design'd;
   By ev'ry beast,
   And creeping thing,
   And fowl of wing,
   His name be blest.
VI.
Let all of royal birth,
With those of humbler frame,
And judges of the earth,
His matchless praise proclaim:
   In this design
   Let youths with maids,

And hoary heads
With children join.
VII.
United zeal be fhown,
His wond'rous fame to raife,
Whofe glorious name alone
Deferves our endlefs praife.
    Earth's utmoft ends
    His pow'r obey:
    His glorious fway
    The fky tranfcends.

PSALM LXII. *Praife to GOD.*

Proper Metre.

I.
PRAISE ye the LORD, the univerfal king,
   His truth and power and his falvation fing,
Him GOD of Gods, him LORD of Lords pro-
                                     [claim,
Let it be known he ever reigns fupreme.
II.
What mighty deeds have by his pow'r been done!
Amazing wonders by his pow'r alone:
He by his wifdom fpread abroad the fky,
And hung out all the ftarry lamps on high.
III.
He bade the feas divide from folid land,
And made the earth above the waters ftand:
He form'd the fun to blefs the day with light,
The moon to cheer the gloomy face of night.

IV.

He for his people needful food provides,
Guards all their blessings, all their steps he guides:
Thro' snares and dangers safely leads them on
To bliss immortal, and his heavenly throne.

PSALM LXIII. *Universal Praise.*

Short Metre.

I.

LET ev'ry creature join
   To praise th' eternal GOD;
Ye heavenly hosts begin the strain
   And sound his name abroad.

II.

Thou sun with golden beams,
   And moon with paler rays,
Ye starry lights, ye heav'nly flames,
   Shine to your maker's praise.

III.

He built those worlds above,
   And fixt their wond'rous frame;
By his command they stand or move,
   And ever speak his name.

IV.

Ye vapours when ye rise,
   Or fall in show'rs or snow,
Ye thunders rolling round the skies,
   His pow'r and glory shew.

V.

Wind, hail, and flashing fire,
   Agree to praise the LORD,

When ye in dreadful ſtorms conſpire
To execute his word.

VI.
By all his works above,
His honours be expreſt;
But ſaints who taſte his ſaving love
Should ſing his praiſes beſt.

PAUSE.

VII.
Ye tribes of Adam join
With heav'n, and earth, and ſeas,
And offer notes divine
To your creator's praiſe.
   Ye holy throng
   Of angels bright,
   In worlds of light
   Begin the ſong.

VIII.
Thou ſun with dazling rays,
And moon that rules the night,
Shine to your maker's praiſe,
With ſtars of twinkling light.
   His pow'r declare,
   Ye floods on high,
   And clouds that fly
   In empty air.

IX.
The ſhining worlds above
In glorious order ſtand,
Or in ſwift courſes move
By his ſupreme command.

He spake the word,
And all their frame
From nothing came
To praise the LORD.

X.

He mov'd their mighty wheels
In unknown ages paſt,
And each his word fulfils
While time and nature laſt.
   In diff'rent ways
   His works proclaim
His wond'rous name,
   And ſpeak his praiſe.

PAUSE.

XI.

Let all the earth-born race,
And monſters of the deep;
The fiſh that cleave the ſeas,
Or in their boſom ſleep,
   From ſea and ſhore
   Their tribute pay,
   And ſtill diſplay
   Their maker's pow'r.

XII.

Ye vapours, hail and ſnow,
Praiſe ye th' almighty LORD,
And ſtormy winds that blow,
To execute his word.
   When lightnings ſhine,
   Or thunders roar,

Let earth adore
His hand divine.

XIII.
Ye mountains near the skies,
With lofty cedars there,
And trees of humbler size,
That fruit in plenty bear;
  Beasts wild and tame,
  Birds, flies and worms,
  In various forms,
  Exalt his name.

XIV.
Ye kings and judges fear
The LORD, the sov'reign king;
And while you rule us here,
His heav'nly honours sing.
  Nor let the dream
  Of pow'r and state,
  Make you forget
  His pow'r supreme.

XV.
Virgins and youths, engage
To sound his praise divine,
While infancy and age
Their feebler voices join.
  Wide as he reigns
  His name be sung,
  By ev'ry tongue,
  In endless strains,

XVI.
Let all the nations fear
The GOD who rules above;

He brings his people near,
And makes them taste his love:
 While earth and sky,
 Attempt his praise,
 His saints shall raise
 His honours high.

Psalm LXIV. *Praise to* GOD.
Long Metre.

I.
O All ye sons of human race,
  Rejoice in heaven's eternal king;
With gladness come before his face,
And Hallelujahs to him sing.

II.
Know that the LORD is GOD supreme,
 By whose all-forming hand alone
Was rais'd from dust our mortal frame;
 We are his flock, he doth us own.

III.
Approach with loud thanksgiving songs,
 The portals of his courts divine,
Laud him to whom all pow'r belongs,
 And to his name your praises join.

IV.
For good and gracious is the LORD,
 His flowing mercy knows no end:
The truth of his most sacred word
 To endless ages shall extend.

PSALM LXV.

Praise to GOD from all Creatures.

Common Metre.

I.

THE glories of our maker GOD
    Our joyful tongues shall sing;
And call the nations to adore
    Their former, and their king.

II.

'Twas his great hand that shap'd our clay,
    And wrought this wond'rous frame:
But from his own celestial breath
    Our nobler spirits came.

III.

We bring our mortal powers to GOD,
    And worship with our tongues:
We claim some kindred with the skies,
    And join the heavenly songs.

IV.

Let beasts which in the pastures feed,
    Or in the desarts lie;
Fishes that move within the seas
    And fowls beneath the sky.

V.

Let rocks, and woods, and fires and seas,
    Their various tribute bring;
And one united homage raise
    To GOD, all nature's king.

VI.

Ye planets to his honour shine,
    As thro' your orbs you run;

Praise him in your eternal course
Around the steady sun.
VII.
The glory of our maker's name,
Thro' all creation flies:
And his unbounded grandeur shines
In worlds beyond the skies.

Psalm LXVI.

Praise for Creation and Providence.

Common Metre.

I.
I Sing th' almighty pow'r of GOD,
That made the mountains rise;
That spread the flowing seas abroad,
And built the lofty skies.

II.
I sing the the wisdom that ordain'd
The sun to rule the day;
The moon shines full at his command,
And all the stars obey.

III.
I sing the goodness of the LORD,
That fill'd the earth with food:
He form'd the creatures with his word,
And then pronounc'd them good.

IV.
LORD, how thy wonders are display'd
Where'er I turn mine eye!

If I survey the ground I tread,
  Or gaze upon the sky.

V.

There's not a plant, or flow'r below,
  But makes thy glories known;
And clouds arise, and tempests blow,
  By order from thy throne.

VI.

Creatures (as num'rous as they be)
  Are subject to thy care:
There's not a place where we can flee,
  But GOD is present there.

VII.

His hand is my prepetual guard,
  He keeps me with his eye:
Why should I then forget the LORD,
  Who is for ever nigh?

PSALM LXVII.

Universal Praise to GOD.

Short Metre.

I.

THY name, almighty LORD,
  Shall sound thro' distant lands:
Great is thy grace, and sure thy word:
  Thy truth for ever stands.

II.

Far be thine honour spread,
  And long thy praise endure,
Till morning light, and ev'ning shade,
  Shall be exchang'd no more.

Psalm LXVIII.

Praise to GOD from all Nations.

Common Metre.

I.

WITH chearful notes let all the earth
 To heav'n their voices raise:
Let all, inspir'd with godly mirth,
 Sing solemn hymns of praise.

II.

GOD's tender mercy knows no bound,
 His truth shall ne'er decay:
Then let the willing nations round
 Their grateful tribute pay.

Psalm LXIX.

Praise to GOD from all Nations.

Common Metre.

I.

O All ye nations, praise the LORD,
 Each with a diff'rent tongue:
In ev'ry language learn his word,
 And let his name be sung.

II.

His mercy reigns thro' ev'ry land;
 Proclaim his grace abroad:
For ever firm his truth shall stand;
 Praise ye the faithful GOD.

Psalm LXX.

Universal Praise to GOD.

Long Metre.

I.

FROM all who dwell below the skies,
  Let the creator's praise arise:
Let the redeemer's name be sung,
Thro' ev'ry land, by ev'ry tongue.

II.

Eternal are thy mercies, LORD;
Eternal truth attends thy word:
Thy praise shall sound from shore to shore,
Till suns shall rise and set no more.

Psalm LXXI. *Praise to GOD.*

Common Metre.

I.

GREAT is the LORD; his works of might
  Demand our noblest songs:
Let his assembled saints unite
  Their harmony of tongues.

II.

Great is the mercy of the LORD,
  He gives his children food;
And ever mindful of his word,
  He makes his promise good.

III.

His son, the great redeemer, came
  To seal his cov'nant sure:

OF PRAISE.

Holy and rev'rend is his name,
   His ways are juſt and pure.

IV.

They who would grow divinely wiſe,
   Muſt with his fear begin;
Our faireſt proof of knowledge lies
   In hating ev'ry ſin.

LXXII. *Praiſe to GOD.*

Long Metre.

I.

PRAISE ye the LORD; our GOD to praiſe
   My ſoul her utmoſt pow'rs ſhall raiſe;
With private friends, and in the throng
Of ſaints, his praiſe ſhall be my ſong.

II.

His works, for greatneſs tho' renown'd,
His wond'rous works with eaſe are found
By thoſe who ſeek for them aright,
And in their pious ſearch delight.

III.

His works are all of matchleſs fame,
And univerſal glory claim:
His truth, confirm'd thro' ages paſt,
Shall to eternal ages laſt.

IV.

By precept he has us enjoyn'd,
To keep his wond'rous works in mind:
And to poſterity record,
That good and gracious is our LORD.

Psalm LXXIII. *Praise to GOD.*

Common Metre.

I.
THEE I will blefs, my GOD and king,
    Thy endlefs praife proclaim;
This tribute daily I will bring,
    And ever blefs thy name.

II.
Thou, LORD, beyond compare art great,
    And highly to be prais'd:
Thy majefty, with boundlefs height,
    Above our knowledge rais'd.

III.
Renown'd for mighty acts, thy fame
    To future times extends:
From age to age thy glorious name
    Succeffively defcends.

IV.
Whilft I thy glory and renown,
    And wond'rous works exprefs:
The world with me thy might fhall own,
    And thy great pow'r confefs.

V.
The praife that to thy love belongs,
    They fhall with joy proclaim:
Thy truth of all their grateful fongs
    Shall be the conftant theme.

VI.
The LORD is good; frefh acts of grace
    His pity ftill fupplies:

His anger moves with flowest pace,
   His willing mercy flies.

VII.

Thy love thro' earth extends its fame,
   To all thy works exprest:
These shew thy praise, whilst thy great name
   Is by thy servants blest.

PSALM LXXIV.

Praise to GOD for his Providence and Grace.

Long Metre.

I.

WITH all my powers of heart and tongue
   I'll praise my maker in my song:
Angels shall hear the notes I raise,
Approve the song, and join the praise.

II.

Angels who make thy church their care
Shall witness my devotions there,
While holy zeal directs my eyes
To thy fair temple in the skies.

III.

I'll sing thy truth and mercy, LORD,
I'll sing the wonders of thy word:
Not all thy works and names below
So much thy pow'r and glory show.

IV.

The GOD of heaven maintains his state,
Frowns on the proud, and scorns the great:
But from his throne descends to see
The sons of humble poverty.

V.

Amidst a thousand snares I stand
Upheld and guarded by thy hand:
Thy words my fainting soul revive,
And keep my dying faith alive.

VI.

Grace will compleat what grace begins,
To save from sorrow or from sins:
The work that wisdom undertakes
Eternal mercy ne'er forsakes.

Psalm LXXV.

Praise to the great and good GOD.

Common Metre.

I.

LONG as we live, we'll bless thy name,
   O king, O GOD of love:
Our work and joy shall be the same,
   In the bright world above.

II.

Great is the LORD, his pow'r unknown,
   And let his praise be great:
We'll sing the honours of thy throne,
   Thy works of grace repeat.

III.

Thy grace shall dwell upon our tongues,
   And while our lips rejoice,
The men who hear our sacred songs,
   Shall join their chearful voice.

of PRAISE.

Fathers to sons shall teach thy name,
  And children learn thy ways:
Ages to come thy truth proclaim,
  And nations found thy praise.

IV.
Thy glorious deeds of antient date
  Shall thro' the world be known:
Thine arm of pow'r, thy heavenly state
  With public splendor shown.

V.
The world is govern'd by thy hands,
  Thy saints are rul'd by love:
And thine eternal kingdom stands,
  Tho' rocks and hills remove.

PSASM LXXVI.

Universal Praise to GOD.

Long Metre.

I.

MY GOD, my King, thy various praise
Shall fill the remnant of my days:
Thy grace employ my humble tongue,
Till death and glory raise the song.

II.
The wings of ev'ry hour shall bear
Some thankful tribute to thine ear:
And every setting sun shall see
New works of duty done for thee.

M

III.

Thy truth and juſtice I'll proclaim;
Thy bounty flows, an endleſs ſtream;
Thy mercy ſwift, thine anger ſlow,
But dreadful to the ſtubborn foe.

IV.

Thy works with ſov'reign glory ſhine,
And ſpeak thy majeſty divine:
Let *Britain* round her ſhores proclaim
The ſound and honour of thy name.

V.

Let diſtant times and nations raiſe
The long ſucceſſion of thy praiſe:
And unborn ages make my ſong
The joy and labour of their tongues.

VI.

But who can ſpeak thy wondrous deeds?
Thy greatneſs all our thoughts exceeds:
Vaſt and unſearchable thy ways,
Vaſt and immortal be thy praiſe.

Psalm LXXVII.

All Creatures called upon to praiſe GOD.

Proper Metre.

I.

O For a hymn of univerſal praiſe!
  Its maker's fame let ev'ry creature raiſe:
Ye lofty heav'ns begin the ſolemn ſound,
And let it ſpread the wide creation round.

II.

Ye angel hoſts who near his dazzling ſeat,
Wrapt in perpetual tranſport humbly wait,

You beſt muſt know the glories of your king,
In ſweeteſt loftieſt ſtrains his wonders ſing.

III.

Bleſs him, thou ſun, great ruler of the day,
Before whoſe ſplendors thine muſt fade away:
To him, the honours paid to thee, reſtore;
And teach mankind thy maker to adore.

IV.

Ye moon and ſtars, who with more feeble light
Break thro' the ſhades, and gild the gloom of night,
Far as you can diffuſe your feeble rays,
Tell his great name, and propagate his praiſe.

PAUSE.

V.

Fair light, the firſt of all created things,
From whom all earthly bliſs and beauty ſprings,
Help the blind world to ſee their maker ſhine
In light eſſential, fairer far than thine.

VI.

Ye dancing ſpheres that ever tuneful move,
Drawn tow'rds your centers by magnetic love,
Convey his name thro' all the vaſt expanſe,
Whilſt to the muſic of his voice you dance.

VII.

Let awful thunders bellowing in the air,
And bluſt'ring ſtorms his dreadful praiſe declare;
Whilſt gentler winds with balmy breath proclaim
The gracious GOD, and ſpread his lovely name.

VIIII.

Let mists, and clouds, and meteors all conspire
In this blest work, and help to fill the choir:
Whilst loud his praises foaming billows roar,
And seas resound his name from shore to shore.

Pause II.

IX.

Ye fertile plains display your gayest pride,
Ye valleys, to his honour, low subside;
And at his call, ye mountains, stately rise,
And bear his praises to the neighbouring skies.

X.

Ye trees of ev'ry kind, ye fruitful vines,
Ye spreading oaks, and tall aspiring pines;
Or bend your heads, or let your juices flow,
To honour him, at whose command you grow.

XI.

To him let ev'ry beast this tribute pay,
He feeds the flocks, he finds the lions prey;
To celebrate his bounty and his pow'r,
Bleat all ye lambs, and all ye lions roar.

XII.

Ye birds, who thro' the airy regions wing,
Nature's musicians, you his praise must sing:
Ye flies and worms, his various skill display;
Tho' you can't sing, this homage you may pay.

Pause III.

XIII.

When nature's all in tune, shall man refrain,
And have his voice and pow'r to sing in vain?

O no! let ev'ry rank, and sex, and age,
With all their might in this design engage.

XIV.
Great kings and potentates, ye gods on earth,
And ev'ry man of meaner rank and birth,
Submit yourselves to his imperial sway,
You're bound, and 'tis your honour to obey.

XV.
Let youthful voices swell th' harmonious choir,
Old age their feebler breath in praise expire:
O! let his love each virgin's heart inflame,
And infants learn to lisp his wond'rous name.

XVI.
But above all, ye saints, your breath employ,
To sound his praises, and to tell your joy:
You, the blest objects of his love and choice,
His glories sing with well tun'd heart and voice.

XVII.
Loud as his thunders let his praises sound,
From heav'n to earth, from world to world rebound:
Let art and nature in the song conspire,
And the whole world become one sacred choir.

Psalm LXXVIII.

Let all in Heaven and Earth praise the LORD.

Long Metre.

I.
O Praise the LORD in that blest place
From whence his goodness largely flows:

Praise him in heav'n where he his face
Unveil'd in perfect glory shews.

II.

Praise him for all the mighty acts,
Which he in our behalf has done:
His kindness this return exacts,
With which our praise should equal run.

III.

Let all who vital breath enjoy,
The breath he does to them afford,
In just returns of praise employ:
Let ev'ry creature praise the LORD.

Psalm LXXIX.

The Instructions of Nature and Success of the Gospel.

Long Metre.

I.

THE heavens declare thy glory, LORD,
In ev'ry star thy wisdom shines:
But when our eyes behold thy word,
We read thy name in fairer lines.

II.

The rolling sun, the changing light,
And nights and days thy pow'r confess:
But the blest volume thou hast writ,
Reveals thy justice and thy grace.

III.

Sun moon and stars convey thy praise
Round the whole earth and never stand:

So when thy truth began its race,
It touch'd and glanc'd on ev'ry land.
IV.
Nor fhall thy fpreading gofpel reft,
Till thro' the world thy truth hath run;
Till Chrift has all the nations bleft,
Who fee the light or feel the fun.

Psalm LXXX.

View of the Heavenly Bodies.

Long Metre.

I.
THE fpacious firmament on high,
With all the blue etherial fky,
And fpangl'd heav'ns, a fhining frame,
Their great original proclaim.
II.
Th' unwearied fun from day to day
Doth his creator's pow'r difplay;
And publifhes to ev'ry land,
The work of one almighty hand.
III.
Soon as the ev'ning fhades prevail,
The moon takes up the wond'rous tale;
And nightly to the lift'ning earth
Repeats the ftory of her birth.
IV.
Whilft all the ftars which round her burn,
And all the planets in their turn,

Confirm the tidings as they roll,
And spread the truth from pole to pole.

V.

What tho' in solemn silence all
Move round the dark terrestial ball;
What tho' no real voice nor sound
Amidst their radiant orbs be found:

VI.

In reason's ear they all rejoice,
And utter forth a glorious voice;
For ever singing as they shine,
The hand which made us is divine.

PSALM LXXXI. *View of Nature,*

Common Metre.

I.

HAIL King supreme! all wise and good,
 To thee our thoughts we raise;
While nature's beauties wide display'd,
 Inspire our souls with praise.

II.

At morning, noon, and ev'ning mild,
 Thy works engage our view;
Oft as we gaze our hearts exult
 With transports ever new.

III.

Thy glory beams in ev'ry star,
 Which gilds the gloom of night:
And decks the rising face of morn
 With rays of cheering light.

IV.

The funny hill the dewy lawn
With thousand beauties shine;
The silent grove, and awful shade
Proclaim thy pow'r divine.

V.

From tree to tree, a constant hymn
Employs the feather'd throng;
To thee their chearful notes they swell,
And chaunt their grateful song.

VI.

Great nature's GOD! still may these scenes
Our serious hours engage;
Still may our grateful hearts consult
Thy works instructive page.

PSALM LXXXII.

View of the Divine Works.

Common Metre.

I.

LOOK round, O man! survey this globe,
    Speak of creating pow'r;
See, nature gives a different robe
    To ev'ry herb and flow'r!

II.

See, various beings fill the air,
    And people earth and sea;
What greatful changes form the year,
    How constant night and day!

III.

Next raiſe thine eye, the vaſt expanſe
 A pow'r unbounded ſhews;
See round the ſun the planets dance,
 And various worlds compoſe.

IV.

Then turn into thy ſelf, O man!
 With wonder view thy ſoul!
Confeſs his pow'r that laid each plan,
 And ſtill directs the whole.

V.

And let obedience to his laws
 Thy gratitude proclaim,
To him the firſt almighty cauſe,
 JEHOVAH is his name.

Psalm LXXXIII.

Thou openeſt thy Hand, they are filled with Good.

Long Metre.

I.

VAST are thy works, almighty LORD,
 All nature reſts upon thy word;
And the whole race of creatures ſtands,
Waiting their portion from thy hands.

II.

While each receives his diff'rent food,
Their chearful looks pronounce it good,
Eagles, and bears, and whales and worms
Rejoice and praiſe in different forms.

III.

But when thy face is hid they mourn,
And dying to their duft return;
Both men and beafts their fouls refign;
Life, breath, and fpirit, all is thine.

IV.

Yet thou can'ft breathe on duft again,
And fill the world with beafts and men;
A word of thy creating breath
Repairs the waftes of time and death.

V.

Thy works, the wonders of thy might,
Are honoured with thy own delight:
How awful are thy glorious ways!
With rev'rence will we fing thy praife.

VI.

The earth ftands trembling at thy ftroke,
And at thy touch the mountains fmoke:
Yet humble fouls may fee thy face,
And tell their wants to fovereign grace.

VII.

In thee our hopes and wifhes meet,
And make our meditations fweet:
Thy praifes fhall our breath employ,
Till it expire in endlefs joy.

PSALM LXXXIV.

View of the Heavens, and Mankind.

Short Metre.

I.

O LORD our heavenly King,
Thy name is all divine;

Thy glories round the earth are spread,
  And o'er the heav'ns they shine.

II.

When to thy works on high,
  I raise my wond'ring eyes,
And see the moon compleat in light
  Adorn the darksome skies:

III.

When I survey the stars
  In all their shining forms,
LORD what is man! of mortal race,
  Akin to dust and worms?

IV.

O LORD our heav'nly king,
  Thy name is all divine,
Thy glories round the earth are spread,
  And thro' the heav'ns they shine.

PSALM LXXXV.

GOD known by his Works.

Long Metre.

I.

GREAT is our GOD, his works of might
  To praise his glorious name unite:
Heav'n, earth and sea confess his hand,
And wait obedient his command.

II.

Thy hand unseen sustains the poles,
On which thy vast creation rolls;

The ſtarry ſkies proclaim thy power,
Thy pencil glows in ev'ry flower.

III.

In various ſhapes and colours riſe
Ten thouſand wonders to our eyes;
And beaſts and birds with labouring throat,
Teach us a GOD in every note.

IV.

A croſs the waves, around the ſky,
There's not a place, or deep or high,
Where the creator has not trod,
And left the footſteps of a GOD.

V.

O may the ſons of men record
The various goodneſs of the LORD,
How vaſt his works, how kind his ways,
And ev'ry tongue pronounce his praiſe.

Psalm LXXXVI.

Works of Creation and Providence.

Common Metre

I.

REJOICE ye righteous in the LORD,
  This work belongs to you;
Sing of his name, his ways, his word,
  How holy, juſt and true.

II.

His mercy and his righteouſneſs,
  Let heav'n and earth proclaim;
His works of nature and of grace
  Reveal his wond'rous name.

III.

His wisdom and almighty word
 The heav'nly arches spread;
And by the spirit of the LORD
 Their shining hosts were made.

IV

He bid the liquid waters flow
 To their appointed deep;
The flowing seas their limits know,
 And their own station keep.

V.

Ye tenants of the spacious earth
 With fear before him stand;
He spake, and nature took its birth,
 And rests on his command.

VI.

Thy glorious works our thoughts engage
 How vast thy pow'r divine!
Thy counsels stand thro' ev'ry age,
 And in full glory shine.

PSALM LXXXVII.

GOD the Lord of Nature.

Long Metre.

I.

WITH glory clad, with strength array'd,
 The LORD, who o'er all nature reigns,
The world's foundations strongly laid,
And the vast fabric still sustains.

II.

How surely stablish'd is thy throne!
Which shall no change or period see';
For thou O LORD, and thou alone,
Art GOD from all eternity.

III.

The floods, O LORD, lift up their voice,
And toss the troubled waves on high;
But GOD above can still their noise,
And make the angry sea comply.

IV.

Thy promise, LORD, is ever sure,
And they who in thy house would dwell,
That happy station to secure,
Must still in holiness excel.

Psalm LXXXVIII.

THANKSGIVING.

Common Metre.

I.

GIVE thanks to GOD, the sov'reign LORD,
  His mercies still endure;
And be the king of kings ador'd,
  His truth is ever sure.

II.

What wonders hath his wisdom done!
  How mighty is his hand;
Heav'n, earth, and sea he fram'd alone,
  How wide is his command.

III.

'The fun fupplies the day with light,
  How bright his counfels fhine!
The moon and ftars adorn the night,
  His works are all divine.

IV.

He faw the nations dead in fin;
  He felt his pity move;
How fad the ftate the world was in!
  How boundlefs was his love.

V.

He fent to fave us from our woe,
  His goodnefs never fails;
From fin and death, and ev'ry foe;
  And ftill his grace prevails.

VI.

Give thanks to GOD our heav'nly king,
  His mercies ftill endure;
Let the whole earth his praifes fing,
  His truth is ever fure.

PSALM LXXXIX.
Thankfgiving.
As the 148th PSALM.

I.

GIVE thanks to GOD moft high,
  The univerfal LORD,
The fov'reign king of kings,
And be his grace ador'd.
  His pow'r and grace
  Are ftill the fame;
  And let his name
  Have endlefs praife.

II.

How mighty is his hand!
What wonders hath he done!
He form'd the earth and feas,
And fpread the heavens alone.
    Thy mercy, LORD,
    Will ftill endure;
    And ever fure
    Abides thy word.

III.

His wifdom fram'd the fun
To blefs the day with light;
The moon and fhining ftars
To cheer the darkfome night.
    His pow'r and grace
    Are ftill the fame;
    And let his name
    Have endlefs praife.

IV.

He faw the nations lie
All perifhing in fin,
And pity'd the fad ftate
The ruin'd world was in.
    Thy mercy, LORD,
    Shall ftill endure;
    And ever fure
    Abides thy word.

V.

He fent his only fon
To fave us from our woe,

From folly, vice, and death,
And ev'ry hurtful foe.
   His pow'r and grace
   Are still the same;
   And let his name
   Have endless praise.

VI.

Give thanks to GOD alone,
To GOD, our heav'nly king,
And let the spacious earth
His boundless goodness sing.
   Thy goodness LORD
   Shall still endure;
   And ever sure
   Abides thy word.

PSALM XC.

Thanksgiving.

Long Metre.

I.

GIVE to our GOD immortal praise!
Mercy and truth are all his ways:
Wonders of grace to GOD belong,
Repeat his mercies in your song.

II.

Give to the LORD of lords renown,
The King of kings with glory crown:
His mercies ever shall endure,
When lords and kings are known no more.

III.

He built the earth, he spread the sky,
And fix'd the starry lights on high:
Wonders of grace to GOD belong,
Repeat his mercies in your song.

IV.

He fills the sun with morning light;
And bids the moon direct the night:
His mercies ever shall endure,
When suns and moons shall shine no more.

V.

He sent his son with pow'r to save,
From guilt and darkness and the grave;
Wonders of grace to GOD belong,
Repeat his mercies in your song.

VI.

Thro' this vain world he guides our feet,
And leads us to his heav'nly seat:
His mercies ever shall endure,
When this vain world shall be no more.

VII.

Give to our GOD immortal praise,
Mercy and truth are all his ways:
Wonders of grace to GOD belong,
Repeat his mercies in your song.

PSALM XCI.

Thanksgiving.

As the 148th PSALM.

I.

TO GOD the mighty LORD,
Your joyful thanks repeat,
To him due praise afford,
As good as he is great:
    For GOD does prove
    Our constant friend;
    His boundless love
    Shall never end.

II.

To him whose wond'rous pow'r
All other gods obey,
Whom earthly kings adore,
This grateful homage pay:
    For GOD does prove
    Our constant friend;
    His boundless love
    Shall never end.

III.

By his almighty hand
Amazing works are wrought;
The heav'ns by his command
Were to perfection brought:
    For GOD does prove
    Our constant friend;
    His boundless love
    Shall never end.

IV.

He spread the ocean round
About the spacious land;
And made the rising ground
Above the waters stand:
> For GOD does prove
> Our constant friend;
> His boundless love
> Shall never end.

V.

Thro' heav'n he did display
His num'rous hosts of light;
The sun to rule by day,
The moon and stars by night:
> For GOD does prove
> Our constant friend;
> His boundless love
> Shall never end.

VI.

[He in our depth of woes,
On us with favour thought,
And from our cruel foes
In peace and safety brought]
> For GOD does prove
> Our constant friend;
> His boundless love
> Shall never end.

VII.

He does the food supply,
On which all creatures live:
To GOD who reigns on high,
Eternal praises give:

For GOD does prove
Our constant friend;
His boundless love
Shall never end.

Psalm XCII.

Thanksgiving, for the Knowledge of GOD, and for Providence.

Common Metre

I.

LET heathens to their idols haste,
   And worship wood and stone;
But our delightful lot is cast
   Where thou, O GOD, art known.

II.

Thy hand provides our constant food,
   And fills our daily cup:
Much are we pleased with present good,
   But more rejoice in hope.

III.

Our souls would all their thoughts approve,
   To thine all-seeing eye,
Nor death, nor hell our hopes shall move,
   While GOD our friend is nigh.

Psalm XCIII.

Thanksgiving, for temporal Blessings.

Long Metre.

I.

WE bless the LORD, the just the good,
   Who fills our hearts with joy and food;

Who pours his bleſſings from the ſkies,
And loads our days with rich ſupplies.

II.

He ſends the ſun his circuit round,
To chear the fruits, to warm the ground:
He bids the clouds with plenteous rain
Refreſh the thirſty earth again.

III.

'Tis to his care we owe our breath,
And all our near eſcapes from death:
Safety and health to GOD belong;
He heals the weak, and guards the ſtrong.

PSALM XCIV.

Thankſgiving.

Common Metre.

I.

SING to the LORD *Jehovah*'s name,
  And in his ſtrength rejoice;
When his ſalvation is our theme,
  Exalted be our voice.

II.

With thanks approach his awful ſight,
  And pſalms of honour ſing;
The LORD's a GOD of boundleſs might,
  The whole creation's king.

III.

Let princes hear, let angels know,
  How mean their natures ſeem;
Thoſe gods on high, and gods below,
  When once compar'd with him.

IV.
Earth with its caverns dark and deep,
 Lies in his fpacious hand;
He fix'd the feas what bounds to keep,
 And where the hills muft ftand.

V.
Come and with humble fouls adore,
 Come kneel before his face;
O may the creatures of his pow'r
 Be children of his grace!

Psalm XCV.

Thanks to GOD for Prefervation.

Common Metre.

I.
TO heav'n I lift my waiting eyes,
 There all my hopes are laid:
The LORD that built the earth and fkies,
 Is my perpetual aid.

II.
Their feet fhall never flide to fall,
 Whom he defigns to keep;
His ear attends the fofteft call;
 His eyes can never fleep.

III.
He will fuftain our weakeft powr's
 With his almighty arm,
And watch our moft unguarded hours
 Againft furprizing harm.

IV.

Ifr'el rejoice, and rest secure,
  Thy keeper is the LORD;
His wakeful eyes employ his pow'r
  For thine eternal guard.

V.

Nor scorching sun, nor sickly moon,
  Shall have its leave to smite;
He shields thy head from burning noon,
  From blasting damps at night.

VI.

He guards thy soul, he keeps thy breath,
  Where thickest dangers come:
Go and return secure from death,
  'Till GOD commands thee home.

Psalm XCVI.

Thanks to GOD our Preserver.

As the 148th Psalm.

I.

UPWARD I lift mine eyes,
  From GOD is all my aid;
The GOD who built the skies,
  And earth and nature made:
    GOD is the tow'r
    To which I fly;
    His grace is nigh
    In ev'ry hour.

II.
My feet shall never slide,
And fall in fatal snares,
Since GOD my guard and guide
Defends me from my fears.
 Those wakeful eyes
 That never sleep,
 Shall *Isr'el* keep,
 When dangers rise.
III.
No burning heats by day,
Nor blasts of ev'ning air,
Shall take my health away,
If GOD be with me there:
 Thou art my sun,
 And thou my shade,
 To guard my head
 By night or noon.
IV.
Hast thou not giv'n thy word
To save my soul from death?
And I can trust my LORD
To keep my mortal breath;
 I'll go and come,
 Nor fear to die.
 Till from on high
 Thou call me home.

Psalm XCVII.

Thanks for temporal and spiritual Mercies.

Long Metre.

I.

GIVE thanks to GOD; he reigns above,
Kind are his thoughts, his name, his love:
His mercy ages paſt have known,
And ages long to come ſhall own.

II.

He feeds and cloaths us ev'ry day,
He guides our footſteps leſt we ſtray;
He guards us with a pow'rful hand,
And brings us to the heav'nly land.

III.

O let the ſaints with joy record,
The truth and goodneſs of the LORD!
How great his works! how kind his ways!
Let ev'ry tongue pronounce his praiſe.

Psalm XCVIII.

GOD's tender Mercy to his People.

Long Metre.

I.

BLESS thou the LORD, my ſoul; his name
Let all the pow'rs within me bleſs:
O let not his paſt favours lie
Forgotten in unthankfulneſs.

II.

'Tis he who pardons all thy sins;
He who,in sickness makes thee sound;
'Tis he redeems thee from the grave;
And still thy life with love is crown'd.

III.

Abundant mercies flow from GOD,
Love is his nature and delight:
Slow is his wrath, and tho' he chides,
His ways are just, his judgments right.

IV.

As heaven is far above the earth,
So his rewards exceed our love;
Farther than east is from the west,
His pardon does our sins remove.

Psalm XCIX.

Give thanks to GOD always in all things.

Long Metre.

I.

GREAT GOD my joyful thanks to thee
Shall, like thy gifts, continual be:
In constant streams thy bounty flows,
Nor end, nor intermission knows.

II.

Thy kindness all my comforts gives,
My num'rous wants thine hand relieves:
Nor can I ever, LORD, be poor,
Who live on thine exhaustless store

III.

If, what I wish, thy will denies,
'Tis because thou art good and wise:
Afflictions, which may make me mourn,
Thou can'st, thou do'st to blessings turn.

IV.

Deep, LORD, upon my thankful breast,
Let all thy favours be imprest;
That I may never more forget
The sum, or any single debt.

V.

May I with grateful heart, each day,
For daily gifts, my praises pay;
Delighted may I always be,
In all things to give thanks to thee.

PSALM C.

Thanksgiving.

Long Metre.

I.

O Render thanks to GOD above,
The fountain of eternal love;
Whose mercy firm thro' ages past
Has stood, and shall for ever last.

II.

Who can his mighty deeds express,
Not only vast, but numberless?
What mortal eloquence can raise,
His tribute of immortal praise?

III.

Happy are they, and only they,
Who from thy judgments never ſtray:
Who know what's right; not only ſo,
But likewiſe practice what they know.

IV.

O may I worthy prove to ſee
Thy ſaints in full proſperity;
That I the joyful choir may join,
And count thy people's triumph mine.

Psalm CI.

Thanks for the Goodneſs of GOD to Mankind.

Common Metre.

I.

O LORD, thy bounty flows above,
    Where all the bleſt reſide;
By thee, the ſpring and life of love,
    With conſtant bliſs ſupplied.

II.

Nor can the heavens extenſive bound
    Thy goodneſs, LORD, confine:
In all thy worlds thy grace is found;
    Earth ſhares in love divine.

III.

But above all thy works below
    Thy creature man is bleſt;
He ſtands, thy great good will to ſhew,
    Diſtinguiſh'd from the reſt.

IV.

With comely form his body's grac'd,
  Tho' for a shell design'd:
But, LORD, how much is this surpass'd
  By his indwelling mind?

V.

There have his nobler pow'rs their seat,
  Which fit him to be blest;
To find in GOD a fund complete
  Of happiness and rest.

VI.

Surprizing love and goodness! LORD,
  That claim our highest praise;
For ever let it be ador'd,
  And holy wonder raise.

Psalm CII.

The Bounty of GOD in the Seasons of the Year.

Proper Tune.

I.

LET thanks to thee, all-sov'reign pow'r arise,
Who fix'd the mountains and who spread the skies;
From the glad climes whence morn in beauty drest,
Forth goes, rejoicing, to the farthest west.

II.

On thee alone our whole dependance lies,
And thy rich mercy ev'ry want supplies:
O thou great author of th' extended whole!
Revolving seasons praise thee as they roll.

III.

By thee, spring, summer, autumn, winter rise,
Thou giv'st the frowning, thou the smiling skies:
By thy command the soft'ning show'r distils,
Till genial warmth the teeming furrow fills.

IV.

Then fav'ring sun-shine o'er the clime extends,
And blest by thee the verdant blade ascends;
Next spring's gay products cloath the flow'ry hills,
And joy the wood, and joy the valley fills.

V.

Then soon thy bounty swells the golden ear,
And bids the harvest crown the fruitful year:
Thus all thy works conspicuous worship raise,
And nature's face proclaims her maker's praise.

Psalm CIII.

Thanks to GOD for his innumerable Mercies

Common Metre

I.

LORD, when I count thy mercies o'er,
    They strike me with surprize;
Not all the sands that spread the shore
    To equal numbers rise.

II.

My flesh with fear and wonder stands,
    The product of thy skill;
And hourly blessings from thy hands
    Thy thoughts of love reveal.

III.

These on my heart by night I keep;
   How kind, how dear to me!
O may the hour that ends my sleep,
   Still find my thoughts with thee.

Psalm CIV.

The Blessings of Spring.

Common Metre.

I.

GOOD is the LORD the heav'nly King,
   Who makes the earth his care;
Visits the pastures ev'ry spring,
   And bids the grass appear.

II.

The clouds, like rivers rais'd on high,
   Pour out, at thy command,
Their wat'ry blessings from the sky,
   To chear the thirsty land.

III.

The soften'd ridges of the field
   Permit the corn to spring;
The vallies rich provision yield,
   And the poor lab'rers sing.

IV.

The little hills, on ev'ry side,
   Rejoice at falling show'rs;
The meadows, dress'd in all their pride,
   Perfume the air with flow'rs.

V.
The barren clods refresh'd with rain,
  Promise a joyful crop;
The parching grounds look green again,
  And raise the reaper's hope.

VI.
The various months thy goodness crowns;
  How bounteous are thy ways?
The bleating flocks spread o'er the downs,
  And shepherds shout thy praise.

Psalm CV.

Hosannah *to* JESUS CHRIST, *the* Saviour.

Common Metre.

I.
HARK the glad sound, the Saviour comes,
  The Saviour promis'd long!
Let ev'ry heart prepare a throne,
  And ev'ry voice a song.

II.
On him the spirit largely pour'd
  Exerts its sacred fire:
Wisdom and might, and zeal and love,
  His holy breast inspire.

III.
He comes the pris'ners to release,
  In Satan's bondage held:
The gates of brass before him burst,
  The iron fetters yeild.

OF THANKSGIVING.

IV.

He came from thickeſt films of vice
　To clear the mental ray;
And on the eye oppreſs'd with night
　To pour celeſtial day.

V.

He comes the broken heart to bind,
　The bleeding foul to cure;
And with the treaſure of his grace,
　T'inrich the humble poor.

VI.

Our glad *Hoſannahs*, Prince of peace,
　Thy welcome ſhall proclaim;
And heaven's eternal arches ring
　With thy beloved name.

PSALM CVI.

Thanks to GOD for Chriſt, and the holy Scriptures.

Long Metre.

I.

GOD, who in various methods told
　His mind and will to ſaints of old,
Sent his own ſon with truth and grace,
To teach us in theſe latter days.

II.

Our nation reads the written word,
That book of life, that true record;
The bright inheritance of heav'n
Is by this ſure conveyance giv'n.

III.

God's kindeſt thoughts are here expreſt,
Able to make us wiſe and bleſt:
The doctrines are divinely true,
Fit for reproof and comfort too.

IV.

O render thanks to GOD above,
For his rich grace, his boundleſs love:
Let all mankind receive his word,
And ev'ry nation praiſe the LORD.

Psalm CVII.

Thanks to GOD for Jesus Christ and the Bleſſings of his Goſpel.

Common Metre.

I.

SING to the LORD, ye diſtant lands,
  Ye tribes of ev'ry tongue;
His new-diſcover'd grace demands
  A new and nobler ſong.

II.

Say to the nations, Jesus reigns,
  GOD's own almighty ſon;
His pow'r the ſinking world ſuſtains,
  And grace ſurrounds his throne.

III.

Let heav'n proclaim the joyful day,
  Joy through the earth be ſeen;
Let cities ſhine in bright array,
  And fields in chearful green.

IV.

Let an unusual joy surprize
　The islands of the sea:
Ye mountains sink, ye valleys rise,
　Prepare the LORD his way.

V.

Behold he comes, he comes to bless
　The nations as their GOD;
To shew the world his righteousness,
　And send his truth abroad.

Psalm CVIII.

Praise for the Gospel.

Common Metre.

I.

TO our almighty maker, GOD,
　New honours be addrest;
His great salvation shines abroad,
　And makes the nations blest.

II.

He spake the word to *Abr'am* first,
　His truth fulfils the grace;
The *gentiles* make his name their trust,
　And learn his righteousness.

III.

Let the whole earth his love proclaim
　With all their diff'rent tongues;
And spread the honours of his name
　In melody and songs.

Psalm CIX.

Thankſgiving for the Bleſſings of the Meſſiah's Kingdom.

Common Metre.

I.

JOY to the world; the LORD is come;
    Let earth receive her king:
Let ev'ry heart prepare him room,
    And heav'n and nature ſing.

II.

Joy to the earth, the SAVIOUR reigns;
    Let men their ſongs employ;
While fields and floods, rocks, hills, and plains,
    Repeat the ſounding joy.

III.

No more let ſins and ſorrows grow,
    Nor thorns infeſt the ground;
He comes to make his bleſſings flow,
    Far as the curſe is found.

IV.

He rules the world with truth and grace,
    And makes the nations prove
The glories of his righteouſneſs,
    And wonders of his love.

PSALM CX.

The Way, and End of the righteous, and wicked.

Common Metre

I.

HOW blest is he, who ne'er confents
  By ill advice to walk;
Nor ftands in finners ways, nor fits
  Where men profanely talk!

II.

But makes the perfect law of GOD
  His bus'nefs and delight;
Devoutly reads therein by day,
  And meditates by night.

III.

Like fome fair tree, which, fed by ftreams,
  With timely fruit does bend;
He ftill fhall flourifh, and fuccefs
  All his defigns attend.

IV.

Ungodly men, and their attempts,
  No lafting root fhall find;
Untimely blafted, and difpers'd
  Like chaff before the wind.

V.

Their guilt fhall ftrike the wicked dumb
  Before their judge's face:
No formal hypocrite fhall then
  Among the faints have place.

VI.

For GOD approves the juſt man's ways;
  To happineſs they tend:
But ſinners, and the paths they tread,
  Shall both in ruin end.

Psalm CXI.

Love to Enemies from the Example of Chriſt.

Common Metre.
I.

GOD of my mercies and my praiſe,
  Thy glory is my ſong;
Tho' ſinners ſpeak againſt thy grace
  With a blaſpheming tongue.

II.

When in the form of mortal man
  Thy ſon on earth was found,
With cruel ſlanders, falſe and vain,
  They compaſs'd him around.

III.

Their mis'ries his compaſſion move,
  Their peace he ſtill purſu'd;
They render hatred for his love,
  And evil for his good.

IV.

Their malice rag'd without a cauſe,
  Yet, with his dying breath,
He pray'd for murd'rers on his croſs,
  And bleſt his foes in death.

V.

LORD, ſhall thy bright example ſhine
  In vain before my eyes?

Give me a soul a-kin to thine,
  To love my enemies.

VI.

The LORD shall on my side engage,
  And, in my Saviour's name,
I shall defeat their pride and rage,
  Who slander and condemn.

Psalm CXII.

The blessed Man.

Proper Tune.

I.

BLEST is the man who fears the LORD,
  And walks with pleasure in his ways,
Who trembles at his holy word,
  Yet gladly his command obeys:
His house with blessings shall abound,
His seed be mighty and renown'd.

II.

A gen'rous pity warms his heart;
His kindness widely he extends;
The poor in all his wealth have part,
To some he gives, to other lends:
Yet what his bounty wastes, repairs
By wisely ord'ring his affairs.

III.

Nor is that lost which he bestows
With lib'ral heart to help the poor;
His hand a future harvest sows,
And scatters to augment his store;

R

His bounty shall himself survive,
And blessings on his heirs derive.

IV.

When times with dismal face appear,
With frightful clouds, and gloom o'er spread,
His heart shall entertain no fear,
Above the gloom he'll lift his head:
His faith shall bear his courage up,
And GOD approves and crowns his hope.

V.

Some friendly beams of cheering light,
Will thro' the darkness make their way;
And in affliction's darkest night,
Their greatest lustre saints display:
That heart ill tidings can't surprize
Which with firm trust on GOD relies.

PSALM CXIII.

The Blessings of the liberal Man.

Proper Tune.

I.

THAT man is blest who stands in awe
Of GOD, and loves his sacred law;
His seed on earth shall be renown'd;
His house the seat of wealth shall be,
An inexhausted treasury,
And with successive honours crown'd.

II.

His lib'ral favours he extends,
To some he gives, to others lends:

A gen'rous pity fills his mind:
Yet what his charity impairs,
He saves by prudence in affairs,
   And thus he's juſt to all mankind.

III.

His hands, while they his alms beſtow'd,
His glory's future harveſt ſow'd:
   The ſweet remembrance of the juſt,
Like a green root, revives and bears
A train of bleſſings for his heirs,
   When dying nature ſleeps in duſt.

IV.

Beſet with threatning dangers round,
Unmov'd ſhall he maintain his ground;
   His conſcience holds his courage up:
The ſoul that's fill'd with virtue's light,
Shines brighteſt in affliction's night;
   And ſees in darkneſs beams of hope.

Psalm CXIV.

Liberality rewarded.

Common Metre.

I.

HAPPY is he who fears the LORD,
   And follows his commands;
Who lends the poor without reward,
   Or gives with lib'ral hands.

II.

As pity dwells within his breaſt
   To all the ſons of need;

So GOD shall answer his request
  With blessings on his seed.

III.

No evil tidings shall surprize
  His well-established mind;
His soul to GOD. his refuge flies,
  And leaves his fears behind.

IV.

In times of general distress
  Some beams of light shall shine,
To shew the world his righteousness,
  And give him peace divine.

V.

His works of piety and love
  Remain before the LORD;
Honour on earth, and joys above,
  Shall be his sure reward.

PSALM CXV.

Brotherly Love.

Long Metre.

I.

O GOD, my Saviour, and my King,
  Of all I have or hope, the spring;
Send down thy spirit from above,
And warm my heart with holy love.

II.

May I from ev'ry act abstain,
That hurts or gives my neighbour pain;

And ev'ry secret wish suppress
That would abridge his happiness,
III.
Still may I feel my heart inclin'd,
To act the friend to all my kind;
Still wish them safety, health and ease,
Wealth, fame, eternal life and peace.
IV.
With mercy let my breath o'erflow,
When I behold a wretch in woe;
And in his sorrows bear a part
With ev'ry one of heavy heart.
V.
But when my neighbour's prosp'rous state,
Shall pleasure in himself create;
Let me too in his triumph join,
Nor once at his success repine.
VI.
With hearty and with forward zeal,
May I promote my brother's weal;
Be pleas'd to please, and give content,
His griefs to ease, or to prevent,
VII.
And shou'd my neighbour spiteful prove,
Still let me vanquish spite with love;
Slow to resent, tho' he would grieve,
But apt and ready to forgive.
VIII.
Let love in all my conduct shine,
An image fair, tho' faint of thine:
Thus I thy follower wou'd prove
Father of men, great *GOD of love*.

Psalm CXVI.

A good Conscience, and Submission to GOD.
Long Metre.
I.

WHILE some in folly's pleasures roll,
And seek the joys which hurt the soul;
Be ours that silent calm repast,
A peaceful conscience to the last:

II.
That tree, which bears immortal fruit,
Without a canker at the root:
That friend, who never fails the just,
When other friends desert their trust.

III.
Amidst the various scene of ills,
Each stroke some kind design fulfills:
And shall we murmur at our GOD,
When sov'reign love directs the rod?

IV.
Though heav'n afflicts, we'll not repine;
We still have peace and joys divine:
Joys which will over death prevail,
And brighten up its gloomy vale.

Psalm CXVII.

The Pleasures of a good Conscience.
Long Metre.
I.

LORD, how secure and blest are they,
Whose hands are pure, whose hearts are clean:

Should tempests shake the earth and sea,
Their minds have heav'n and peace within.

II.
The day glides sweetly o'er their head,
Made up of innocence and love:
And soft and silent as the shades,
Their nightly minutes gently move.

III.
Quick as their thoughts their joys come on,
But fly not half so fast away:
Their souls are ever bright as noon,
And calm as summer ev'nings be.

IV.
How oft they look to th' heavenly hills,
Where groves of living pleasure grow?
And pleasing hopes, and chearful smiles
Sit undisturb'd upon their brow.

V.
They scorn to pine for golden toys,
But spend the day, and share the night,
In musing o'er diviner joys,
Which heaven prepares for their delight.

PSALM CXVIII.

The Pleasures of domestic Friendship.

Short Metre.

I.

BLEST are the sons of peace,
    Whose hearts and hopes are one;
Whose kind designs to serve and please
    Thro' all their actions run.

II.

Bleſt is the pious houſe
　Where zeal and friendſhip meet;
Their ſongs of praiſe, their mingled vows,
　Make their communion ſweet.

III.

Thus when on *Aaron*'s head
　They pour'd the rich perfume,
The oil thro' all his raiment ſpread,
　And pleaſure fill'd the room.

IV.

Thus on the heav'nly hills
　The ſaints are bleſt above,
Where joy like morning-dew diſtils,
　And all the air is love.

Psalm CXIX.

Common Metre.

Humility and Submiſſion.

I.

IS there ambition in my heart?
　Search, gracious GOD, and ſee;
Or do I act a haughty part?
　LORD, I appeal to thee.

II.

I charge my thoughts, be humble ſtill,
　And all my carriage mild,
Content, my father, with thy will,
　And quiet as a child.

III.

The patient foul, the lowly mind,
  Shall have a large reward:
Let faints in forrow lie refign'd,
  And truft a faithful LORD.

Psalm CXX.

Obedience is better than Sacrifice.

Common Metre.

I.

THUS faith the LORD, "the fpacious fields,
  " And flocks and herds are mine;
" O'er all the cattle of the hills
  " I claim a right divine.

II.

" I afk no fheep for facrifice,
  " Nor bullocks burnt with fire;
" To hope and love, to pray and praife,
  " Is all that I require.

III.

" Call upon me when trouble's near,
  " My hand fhall fet thee free;
" Then fhall thy thankful lips declare
  " The honour due to me.

IV.

" The man who offers humble praife,
  " He glorifies me beft;
" And thofe who tread my holy ways
  " Shall my falvation tafte.

S

DEVOTIONAL

Psalm CXXI.

The Happiness of a virtuous Life.

Common Metre.

I.

HOW bless'd are they who always keep
   The pure and perfect way!
Who never from the sacred paths
   Of GOD's commandments stray!

II.

How bless'd! who to his righteous laws
   Have still obedient been!
And have with fervent humble zeal
   His favour sought to win!

III.

Such men their utmost caution use
   To shun each wicked deed;
But in the path which he directs
   With constant care proceed.

IV.

Thou strictly hast enjoin'd us, LORD,
   To learn thy sacred will;
And all our diligence employ
   Thy statutes to fulfil.

V.

O then that thy most holy will
   Might o'er my ways preside!
And I the course of all my life
   By thy direction guide!

VI.

Then with affurance fhould I walk,
  From all confufion free;
Convinc'd, with joy, that all my ways
  With thy commands agree.

Psalm CXXII.

Going to Church.

Proper Tune.

I.

HOW pleas'd and bleft was I,
  To hear the people cry,
Come, let us feek our GOD to-day;
  Yes, with a chearful zeal
  We hafte to *Zion*'s hill,
And there our vows and honours pay.

II.

Zion, thrice happy place,
  Adorn'd with wond'rous grace,
And walls of ftrength embrace thee round;
  In thee our tribes appear
  To pray, and praife, and hear,
The facred gofpel's joyful found.

III.

May peace attend thy gate,
  And joy within thee wait,
To blefs the foul of ev'ry gueft;
  The man who feeks thy peace,
  And wifhes thine increafe,
A thoufand bleffings on him reft!

IV.

My tongue repeats her vows,
"*Peace to this sacred house!*
For there my friends and kindred dwell;
And since my glorious GOD
Makes thee his best abode,
My soul shall ever love thee well.

Psalm CXXIII.

Instruction from Scripture.

Common Metre.

I.

HOW shall the young secure their hearts,
　And guard their lives from sin?
Thy word the choicest rules imparts
　To keep the conscience clean.

II.

When once it enters to the mind,
　It spreads such light abroad,
The meanest souls instruction find,
　And raise their thoughts to GOD.

III.

'Tis like the sun, a heav'nly light,
　That guides us all the day;
And thro' the dangers of the night,
　A lamp to lead our way.

IV.

The men who keep thy law with care,
　And meditate thy word,

Grow wiſer than their teachers are,
  And better know the LORD.

V.
Thy precepts make me truly wiſe;
  I hate the ſinner's road:
I hate my own vain thoughts that riſe,
  But love thy law, my GOD.

VI.
[The ſtarry heav'ns thy rule obey,
  The earth maintains her place;
And theſe thy ſervants night and day
  Thy ſkill and pow'r expreſs.

VII.
But ſtill thy law and goſpel, LORD,
  Have leſſons more divine:
Not earth ſtands firmer than thy word,
  Nor ſtars ſo nobly ſhine.]

VIII.
Thy word is everlaſting truth,
  How pure is ev'ry page!
That holy book ſhall guide our youth,
  And well ſupport our age.

PSALM CXXIV.

The Character and Hope of the good Man.

Common Metre.

I.
LORD, who's the happy man who may
    To thy bleſt courts repair;
Not, ſtranger-like, to viſit them,
   But to inhabit there?

DEVOTIONAL

II.
'Tis he, whose ev'ry thought and deed
  By rules of virtue moves;
Whose gen'rous tongue disdains to speak
  The thing his heart disproves.

III.
Who never did a slander forge,
  His neighbour's fame to wound;
Nor hearken to a false report,
  By malice whisper'd round.

IV.
Who vice, in all its pomp and pow'r,
  Can treat with just neglect;
And piety, tho' cloath'd in rags,
  Religiously respect.

V.
Who to his plighted vows and trust
  Has ever firmly stood;
And tho' he promise to his loss,
  He makes his promise good.

VI.
Whose soul in sinful ways disdains
  His treasure to employ;
Whom no rewards can ever bribe
  The guiltless to destroy.

VII.
The man, who by this steady course
  Has happiness insur'd:
When earth's foundation shakes, shall stand,
  By providence secur'd.

Psalm CXXV.

The Excellency of the Gospel.

Short Metre.

I.
BEHOLD the morning sun
  Begins his glorious way;
His beams thro' all the nations run,
  And life and light convey.

II.
But where the Gospel comes,
  It spreads diviner light;
It calls dead sinners from their tombs,
  And gives the blind their sight.

III.
How perfect is thy word,
  And all thy judgments just;
For ever sure thy promise LORD,
  And men securely trust.

IV.
My gracious GOD how plain,
  Are thy directions giv'n;
O may I never read in vain,
  But find the path to heav'n.

V.
While with my heart and tongue,
  I spread thy praise abroad,
Accept the worship and the song,
  My SAVIOUR and my GOD.

Psalm CXXVI.

The Excellency of the Scriptures.

As the 113 Psalm.

I.

I Love the volumes of thy word;
What light and joy those leaves afford
To souls benighted and distrest!
Thy precepts guide my doubtful way,
Thy fear forbids my feet to stray,
Thy promise leads my heart to rest.

II.

From the discov'ries of thy law
The perfect rules of life I draw,
These are my study and delight:
Not honey so invites the taste,
Nor gold that hath the furnace past,
Appears so pleasing to the sight.

III.

Thy threat'nings wake my slumb'ring eyes,
And warn me where my danger lies;
But 'tis thy blessed Gospel, LORD,
That makes my guilty conscience clean,
Converts my soul, subdues my sin,
And gives a free, but large reward.

IV.

Who knows the errors of his thoughts?
My GOD, forgive my secret faults,
And from presumptuous sins restrain:
Accept my poor attempts of praise,
That I have read thy book of grace,
And book of nature, not in vain.

PSALMS.

Psalm CXXVII.

The Pleaſure of Public Worſhip.

Long Metre.

I.

How pleaſant, how divinely fair,
O LORD of hoſts, thy dwellings are!
With long deſire my ſpirit faints
To meet the aſſemblies of thy ſaints.

II.

My fleſh would reſt in thine abode,
My panting heart cries out for GOD:
My GOD! my King! why ſhould I be
So far from all my joys and thee?

III.

Bleſt are the ſaints who ſit on high
Around thy throne of majeſty:
Thy brighteſt glories ſhine above,
And all their work is praiſe and love.

IV.

Bleſt are the ſouls who find a place
Within the temple of thy grace;
There they behold thy gentler rays.
And ſeek thy face, and learn thy praiſe.

V.

Bleſt are the men whoſe hearts are ſet
To find the way to *Zion*'s gate:
GOD is their ſtrength; and thro' the road
They lean upon their helper, GOD.

T

VI.

Chearful they walk with growing strength,
'Till all shall meet in heav'n at length;
'Till all before thy face appear,
And join in nobler worship there.

PSALM CXXVIII.

Sincerity in Divine Worship.

Common Metre.

I.

GOD is a spirit, just and wise,
   He sees our inmost mind:
In vain to heav'n we raise our cries,
   And leave our souls behind.

II.

Nothing but truth before his throne,
   With honour can appear:
The formal hypocrites are known,
   Thro' the disguise they wear.

III.

Their lifted eyes salute the skies,
   Their bending knees the ground:
But GOD abhors the sacrifice,
   Where not the heart is found.

IV.

LORD search our thoughts, and try our ways,
   And make our souls sincere:
Then shall we stand before thy face,
   And find acceptance there.

PSALMS.

Psalm CXXIX.

The Life and Death of good Men.

Common Metre.

I.

MY GOD, the steps of pious men
  Are order'd by thy will;
Tho' they shou'd fall, they rise again;
  Thy hand supports them still.

II.

The LORD delights to see their ways,
  Their virtue he approves;
He'll ne'er deprive them of his grace,
  Or leave the man he loves.

III.

The heavenly heritage is theirs,
  Their portion and their home:
He feeds them now, and makes them heirs
  Of blessings long to come.

IV.

Mark well the man of righteousness,
  His sev'ral steps attend;
True pleasure runs thro' all his ways,
  And peaceful is his end.

Psalm CXXX.

The Justice and Goodness of GOD.

Common Metre.

I.

THY justice, LORD, maintains its throne,
  Tho' mountains melt away;

Thy judgments are a world unknown,
  A deep unfathom'd fea.

II.

Safety to men thy goodnefs brings,
  Nor overlooks the beaft:
Beneath the fhadow of thy wings
  Thy children love to reft.

III.

From thee, when fhort-liv'd joys run low,
  And mortal comforts die;
Perpetual fprings of life fhall flow,
  And raife our pleafures high.

IV.

Tho' all created light decay,
  And death clofe up our eyes;
Thy prefence makes eternal day,
  Where clouds can never rife.

Psalm CXXXI.

The Character and Reward of the good Man.

Long Metre.

I.

THIS fpacious earth is all the LORD's,
  And men, and worms, and beafts, and birds;
He rais'd it high above the feas,
And form'd it for their dwelling place.

II.

But there's a brighter world on high,
The heav'nly feats above the fky:
Who fhall afcend that bleft abode,
And dwell fo near his maker GOD?

III.

He who abhors, and fears to fin,
Whofe heart is pure; whofe hands are clean:
Him will the LORD delight to blefs,
And cloath with robes of righteoufnefs.

IV.

Thefe are the men, the pious race,
Who feek their heav'nly fathers face;
Thefe fhall enjoy the blifsful fight,
And dwell in everlafting light.

Psalm CXXXII.

The Seafons of the Year.

Common Metre.

I.

WITH fongs and honours founding loud
    Addrefs the LORD on high;
Over the heav'ns he fpreads his cloud,
  And waters veil the fky.

II.

He fends his fhow'rs of bleffings down
  To chear the plains below:
He makes the grafs the mountains crown,
  And corn in valleys grow.

III.

He gives the grazing ox his meat,
  He hears the ravens cry:
But man who taftes his fineft wheat,
  Should raife his honours high.

IV.

His steady counsels change the face,
   Of the declining year;
He bids the sun cut short his race,
   And wint'ry days appear.

V.

His hoary frost, his fleecy snow,
   Descend and clothe the ground;
The liquid streams forbear to flow,
   In icy fetters bound.

VI.

When from his dreadful stores on high
   He pours the rattling hail,
The wretch that dares his GOD defy
   Shall find his courage fail.

VII.

He sends his word and melts the snow,
   The fields no longer mourn;
He calls the warmer gales to blow,
   And bids the spring return.

VIII.

The changing wind, the flying cloud,
   Obey his mighty word:
With songs and honours sounding loud,
   Praise ye the sov'reign LORD.

PSALM CXXXIII.

The Citizen of Zion.

Common Metre.

I.

WHO shall inhabit in thy hill,
   O GOD of holiness?

Whom will the LORD admit to dwell
  So near his throne of grace?
II.
The man who walks in pious ways,
  And works with right'ous hands;
Who trusts his maker's promises,
  And follows his commands.
III.
He speaks the meaning of his heart,
  Nor flanders with his tongue;
Will scarce believe an ill report,
  Nor do his neighbour wrong.
IV.
The wealthy sinner he contemns,
  Loves all who fear the LORD;
And tho' to his own hurt he swears,
  Still he performs his word.
V.
His hands disdain a golden bribe,
  And never gripe the poor:
This man shall dwell with GOD on earth,
  And find his heav'n secure.

Psalm CXXXIV.

Seeking after GOD.

Short Metre.

I.
MY GOD, permit my tongue
  This joy, to call thee mine;
And let my early cries prevail
  To taste thy love divine.

II.

For life, without thy love,
  No relish can afford:
No joy can be compar'd to this,
  To serve and please the LORD.

III.

To thee I'll lift my hands,
  And praise thee while I live;
Not all the dainties of a feast,
  Such food or pleasure give.

IV.

In wakeful hours of night,
  I call my GOD to mind;
I think how wise thy counsels are,
  And all thy dealings kind.

V.

Since thou hast been my help,
  To thee my spirit flies;
And on thy watchful providence
  My chearful hope relies.

VI.

The shadow of thy wings
  My soul in safety keeps:
I follow where my father leads,
  And he supports my steps.

PSALM CXXXV.

For Blessing of GOD on the Business and Comforts of Life.

Long Metre.

I.

IF GOD succeed not, all the cost
  And pains to build the house are lost,

If GOD the city will not keep,
The watchful guards as well may sleep.

II.
What if you rise before the sun,
And work and toil when day is done;
Careful and sparing eat your bread,
To shun the poverty you dread:

III.
'Tis all in vain, till GOD hath blest;
He can make rich, yet give us rest:
Children and friends are blessings too,
If GOD our sov'reign make them so.

IV.
Happy the man to whom he sends
Obedient children, faithful friends!
How sweet our daily comforts prove
When they are season'd with his love!

Psalm CXXXVI.

Breathing after Holiness.

Common Metre.

I.
O That the LORD would guide my ways
    To keep his statutes still!
O that my GOD would grant me grace
    To know and do his will.

II.
O send thy spirit down to write
    Thy law upon my heart!

U

Nor let my tongue indulge deceit,
　　Nor act the liar's part.

III.
From vanity turn off my eyes,
　　Let no corrupt design,
Nor covetous desires arise
　　Within this soul of mine.

IV.
Order my footsteps by thy word,
　　And make my heart sincere;
Let sin have no dominion, LORD,
　　But keep my conscience clear.

V.
My soul hath gone too far astray,
　　My feet too often slip;
Yet since I've not forgot thy way,
　　Restore thy wand'ring sheep.

VI.
Make me to walk in thy commands;
　　'Tis a delightful road:
Nor let my head, or heart, or hands,
　　Offend against my GOD.

PSALM CXXXVII.

The true Way to please GOD.

Common Metre.

I.
WHEREWITH shall I approach the LORD,
　　And bow before his throne?
Or how procure his kind regard,
　　And for my guilt atone?

II.
Shall altars flame, and victims bleed,
  And spicy fumes ascend?
Will these my earnest wish succeed,
  And make my GOD my friend?
III.
Should thousand rams in flames expire,
  Would these his favours buy?
Or oil that should, for holy fire,
  Ten thousand streams supply?
IV.
With trembling hands, and bleeding heart,
  Should I mine offspring slay:
Would this atone for ill-desert,
  And purge my guilt away?
V.
Oh! no, my soul, 'twere fruitless all,
  Such victims bleed in vain:
No fatlings from the field or stall,
  Such favours can obtain.
VI.
To men their *rights* I must allow,
  And proofs of *kindness* give:
To GOD with *humble rev'rence* bow,
  And to his glory live.
VII.
Hands that are clean, and hearts sincere,
  He never will despise:
And chearful duty he'll prefer
  To costly sacrifice.

DEVOTIONAL

PSALM CXXXVIII.

Heavenly Joy on Earth, and Prospect of Immortality.

Short Metre.

I.

COME, we who love the LORD,
  And let our joys be known;
Join in a song with sweet accord,
  And thus surround the throne.

II.

The sorrows of the mind
  Be banish'd from the place;
Religion never was design'd
  To make our pleasures less.

III.

The GOD who rules on high,
  And thunders when he please,
Who rides upon the stormy sky,
  And manages the seas:

IV.

This awful GOD is ours,
  Our father, and our love,
He shall send down his heav'nly pow'r
  To carry us above

V.

Then shall we see his face,
  And never, never sin;
There from the rivers of his grace
  Drink endless pleasures in.

VI.

Yes, and before we rife
 To that immortal flate,
The thoughts of fuch amazing blifs
 Should conftant joys create.

VII.

The men of grace have found
 Glory begun below:
Celeftial fruits, on earthly ground,
 From faith and hope may grow.

VIII.

Then let our fongs abound,
 And ev'ry tear be dry;
We're marching thro' *Immanuel*'s, ground
 To fairer worlds on high.

Psalm CXXXXIX.

Men called upon to worship GOD.

Short Metre.

I.

COME, found his praife abroad,
 And hymns of glory fing:
Jehovah is the fov'reign GOD,
 The univerfal King.

II.

He form'd the deeps unknown;
 He gave the feas their bound;
The wat'ry worlds are all his own,
 And all the folid ground.

III.

Come, worſhip at his throne,
  Come bow before the LORD;
We are his works, and not our own,
  He form'd us by his word.

IV.

To day attend his voice,
  Nor dare provoke his rod;
Come, like the people of his choice,
  And own your gracious GOD.

Psalm CXL.

Bleſſed are the Dead, who die in the LORD.

Common Metre.

I.

HARK! from on high a chearing voice,
  Lend all a liſt'ning ear:
'Twill make each pious heart rejoice,
  And vanquiſh ev'ry fear,

II.

" Write hence forth, bleſſed are the dead
  " Who in the LORD ſhall die: .
" Their weary fleſh, as on a bed,
  " Soft in a grave ſhall lie.

III.

" Whilſt their glad ſouls, at laſt releas'd,
  " To heav'n ſhall take their flight!
" There to enjoy eternal reſt,
  " And infinite delight.

IV.
" They'll drop each load as they afcend,
  " And bid farewell to woe:
" Their labours with their lives fhall end,
  " Their reft no period know.
V.
" They'll drudge no more for daily bread,
  " No more of fin complain;
" No more be pinch'd with any need,
  " Nor griev'd with any pain.
VI.
" Their conflicts then with bufy foes,
  " For evermore fhall ceafe:
" None fhall their pleafing work oppofe,
  " Or once difturb their peace.
VII.
" But vaft rewards fhall recompence
  " Their hearty fervice here:
" And perfect love fhall banifh thence,
  " All diffidence and fear.

Psalm CXLI.

New Year's Day.

Common Metre.

I.

AND now, my foul, another year,
    Of my fhort life is paft:
I cannot long continue here,
    And this may be my laft.

DEVOTIONAL

II.

Much of my dubious life is done,
 Nor will return again:
And with my passing moments run,
 The few that yet remain.

III.

Awake, my soul, with utmost care
 Thy true condition learn:
What are thy hopes, how sure, how fair?
 And what thy chief concern?

IV.

Now a new scene of time begins,
 Set out therewith for heav'n:
Repent of all thy former sins,
 Reform, and be forgiv'n.

V.

Devoutly yield thyself to GOD,
 And to his care commend:
With zeal pursue the heav'nly road,
 Nor doubt an happy end.

Psalm CXLII.

The LORD is our Shepherd.

As the 113 Psalm.

I.

THE LORD my pasture shall prepare,
 And feed me with a shepherd's care:
His presence shall my wants supply,
And guard me with a watchful eye;
My noon-day walks he shall attend,
And all my midnight hours defend.

II.

When in the fultry glebe I faint,
Or on the thirfty mountain pant;
To fertile vales and dewy meads
My weary wand'ring fteps he leads;
Where peaceful rivers foft and flow
Amid the verdant landfcape flow.

III.

Tho' in the paths of death I tread,
With gloomy horrors over-fpread,
My ftedfaft heart fhall fear no ill,
For thou, O LORD, art with me ftill;
Thy friendly hand fhall give me aid,
And guide me thro' the dreadful fhade.

IV.

Tho' in a bare and rugged way,
Thro' devious lonely wilds I ftray,
Thy bounty fhall my pains beguile,
The barren wildernefs fhall fmile,
With fudden greens and herbage crown'd;
And ftreams fhall murmur all around.

Psalm CXLIII.

The LORD's Prayer imitated.

Common Metre.

I.

FATHER of all! eternal Mind!
   Immenfely good and great!
Thy children form'd and blefs'd by thee,
   Approach thy heav'nly feat.

II.

Thy name in hallow'd strains be sung!
  We join the solemn praise:
To thy great name, with heart and tongue,
  Our chearful homage raise.

III.

Thy righteous, mild, and sov'reign reign
  Let ev'ry being own:
And in our minds, thy work divine,
  Erect thy gracious throne.

IV.

As angels round thy seat above,
  Thy blest commands fulfil;
So may thy creatures here below
  Perform thy heav'nly will.

V.

On thee we day by day depend,
  Our daily wants supply:
And feed with truth and virtue pure,
  Our souls which never die.

VI.

Extend thy grace to every fault,
  Oh! let thy love forgive:
Teach us divine forgiveness too,
  Nor let resentments live.

VII.

Where tempting snares bestrew the way,
  Permit us not to tread:
Avert the threat'ning evil near,
  From our unguarded head.

VIII.

Thy sacred name we thus adore,
  With joyful humble mind:
And praise thy goodness, power, and truth,
  Eternal, unconfin'd.

Psalm CXLIV.

For Christmas Day.

Proper Tune.

I.

ARISE, and hail the happy day;
  Cast all low cares of life away,
    And thought of meaner things:
This day to cure our deadly woes,
The sun of righteousness arose,
  With healing in his wings.

II.

If angels on that happy morn,
The Saviour of the world was born,
  Pour'd forth their joyful songs;
Much more shou'd we of human race,
Adore the wonders of his grace,
  To whom the grace belongs.

III.

How wonderful! how vast his love!
Who left the shining realms above,
  Those happy seats of rest!
How much for human-kind he bore,
Their peace and pardon to restore,
  Can never be express'd.

IV.

Whilſt we adore his boundleſs grace,
And holy joy and thanks take place
   Of ſorrow, grief, and pain;
Give glory to our GOD moſt high,
And not amongſt the gen'ral joy,
   Forget good will to men.

V.

O then let heav'n and earth rejoice,
Creation's whole united voice,
   And hymn the happy day;
When *Satan*'s empire vanquiſh'd fell,
And all the pow'rs of death and hell,
   Before his ſov'reign ſway.

Psalm CXLV.

A public national Thankſgiving.

As the 113 Psalm.

I.

SAY, ſhould we ſearch the globe around,
Where can ſuch happineſs be found,
   As dwells in Britain's favour'd iſle?
Here plenty reigns; here freedom ſheds
Her choiceſt bleſſings on our heads,
   And bids our bleakeſt mountains ſmile.

II.

Here commerce ſpreads the wealthy ſtore
That comes from ev'ry foreign ſhore;
   Science and art their charms diſplay;

Religion teaches us to raise
Our voices to our maker's praise,
   As truth and conscience point the way.

III.

When FRANCE, from pride and envy, plann'd
The ruin of our blissful land,
   Here vict'ry arm'd her chosen race;
Go forth, my valiant sons, she said,
Go strike the haughty GAUL with dread,
   And triumph in his deep disgrace.

IV.

These are thy gifts, almighty King!
From thee our matchless blessings spring:
   Th' extended trade, the fruitful skies,
The raptures liberty bestows,
Th' eternal joys the gospel shews,
   All from thy boundless goodness rise.

V.

From thee, the zeal and spirit came,
That did our patriot chiefs inflame;
   Their skill, their courage, all are thine:
Our daring troops with glory crown'd,
Tell to the wond'ring nations round,
   The hand that leads us is divine.

VI.

With grateful hearts, with gladsome tongues,
To GOD we raise triumphant songs;
   His pow'r, his mercy, we proclaim:
At length, ye faithless tyrants, own
JEHOVAH here hath fix'd his throne,
   And tremble at his awful name.

VII.

Long as the moon her courſe ſhall run,
Or man behold the circling ſun,
  O ſtill may GOD in BRITAIN reign!
Still crown her armies with ſucceſs,
With peace and joy her borders bleſs,
  And all her ſacred rights maintain.

PSALM CXLVI.

A Morning Pſalm.

Common Metre.

I.

ON thee, each morning, O my GOD,
  My waking thoughts attend;
In whom are founded all my hopes,
  And all my wiſhes end.

II.

My ſoul, in pleaſing wonder loſt,
  His boundleſs love ſurveys;
And, fir'd with grateful zeal, prepares,
  Her ſacrifice of praiſe.

III.

He leads me thro' the maze of ſleep,
  He brings me ſafe to light;
And, with the ſame paternal care,
  Conducts my ſteps till night.

IV.

When ev'ning ſlumbers preſs my eyes,
  With his protection bleſt,
In peace and ſafety I commit,
  My weary'd limbs to reſt.

V.

My spirit, in his hands secure,
 Fears no approaching ill;
For, whether waking or asleep,
 The LORD is with me still.

VI.

I'll daily to th' astonish'd world,
 His wond'rous acts proclaim;
While all with me shall praises sing,
 With me shall bless his name.

VII.

At morn, and noon, and night I'll still
 The growing work pursue;
And him alone will praise, to whom
 Eternal praise, is due.

Psalm CXLVII.

An Evening Psalm.

Common Metre.

I.

INDULGENT GOD, whose bount'ous care
 O'er all thy works is shewn!
Oh! let my grateful pray'r and praise
 Ascend before thy throne.

II.

What mercies has this day bestow'd,
 How largely hast thou blest!
My cup with plenty overflow'd,
 With chearfulness my breast.

III.

Now may sweet slumbers close my eyes,
 From pain and sickness free;

And let my waking thoughts arife
To meditate on thee.

IV.

So blefs each future day and night,
Till life's fond fcene is o'er;
And then to realms of endlefs light,
O! let my fpirit foar.

PSALM CXLVIII.

The Pleafures of Divine Worſhip.

Proper Tune.

I.

LORD of the worlds above,
How pleafant and how fair
The dwellings of thy love,
Thy earthly temples are:
To thine abode
My heart afpires,
With warm defires
To fee my GOD.

II.

The fparrow for her young
With pleafure feeks a neft,
And wand'ring fwallows long
To find their wonted reft;
My fpirit faints
With equal zeal
To rife and dwell
Among thy faints.

III.

O happy fouls that pray,
Where GOD appoints to hear!
O happy men that pay
Their conſtant ſervice there!
 They praiſe thee ſtill;
 And happy they
 That love the way
 To *Zion*'s hill.

IV.

They go from ſtrength to ſtrength,
Thro' this dark vale of tears,
Till each arrives at length,
Till each in heav'n appears:
 O glorious ſeat,
 When GOD our King
 Shall thither bring
 Our willing feet!

PAUSE.

V.

To ſpend one ſacred day
Where GOD and ſaints abide,
Affords diviner joy
Than thouſand days beſide:
 Where GOD reſorts
 I love it more
 To keep the door
 Than ſhine in courts.

VI.

GOD is our ſun and ſhield,
Our light and our defence;

Y

With gifts his hands are fill'd,
We draw our blessings thence;
  He shall bestow
  On *Jacob*'s race
  Peculiar grace
  And glory too.

VII.

The LORD his people loves;
His hand no good with-holds
From those his heart approves,
From pure and pious souls:
  Thrice happy he,
  O GOD of hosts,
  Whose spirit trusts
  Alone in thee.

Psalm CXLIX.

Universal Prayer.

Common Metre.

I.

FATHER of all! in ev'ry age,
  In ev'ry clime ador'd,
By saint, by savage, and by sage,
  JEHOVAH, JOVE, or LORD!

II.

What conscience dictates to be done,
  Or warns me not to do,
This, teach me more than hell to shun,
  That, more than heav'n pursue.

III.

What blessings thy free bounty gives,
  Let me not cast away;

For GOD is paid when man receives,
  T' enjoy is to obey.

IV.
Yet not to earth's contracted span
  Thy goodness let me bound,
Or think thee LORD alone of man,
  When thousand worlds are round.

V.
Let not this weak unknowing hand
  Presume thy bolts to throw,
And deal damnation round the land,
  On each I judge thy foe.

VI.
If I am right, O teach my heart
  Still in the right to stay;
If I am wrong, thy grace impart
  To find that better way.

VII.
Save me alike from foolish pride,
  Or impious discontent,
At ought thy wisdom has denied,
  Or ought thy goodness lent.

VIII.
Teach me to feel another's woe;
  To hide the fault I see;
That mercy I to others show,
  That mercy show to me.

IX.
Mean tho' I am, not wholly so,
  Since quicken'd by thy breath:
Oh lead me wheresoe'er I go,
  Thro' this day's life or death.

X.

This day be bread and peace my lot;
  All elſe beneath the ſun
Thou know'ſt if beſt beſtow'd or not,
  And let thy will be done,

XI.

To thee whoſe temple is all ſpace,
  Whoſe altar, earth, ſea, ſkies,
One chorus let all beings raiſe!
  All nature's incenſe riſe.

Psalm CL.

Univerſal Praiſe.

Proper Tune.

I.

O Azure vaults! O cryſtal ſky!
  The world's tranſparent canopy,
Break your long ſilence, and let mortals know,
With what contempt you look on things below.

II.

O light! the faireſt, firſt of things,
  From whom all joy, all beauty ſprings,
Praiſe the almighty ruler of the globe
Who uſeth thee for his imperial robe.

III.

Thou radiant ſun! whoſe glorious ray
  Rules the bright empire of the day:
O praiſe his name, without whoſe purer light
Thou hadſt been hid in an abyſs of night.

IV.

Ye moon and planets! who diſpence
  By GOD's command, your influence:

Vaſt ever-moving orbs; exalt his name
Who gave its being to each glorious frame.

V.

Ye miſts and vapours, hail and ſnow,
And you who thro' the concave blow
Swift executors of his holy word,
Whirlwinds, and tempeſts, praiſe th' almighty LORD.

VI.

Mountains, who to your maker's view
Are leſs than mole-hills ſeem to you,
Praiſe him, who did all forms from chaos draw,
Him whoſe command is univerſal law.

VII.

Praiſe him ye monſters of the deep
That in the ſea's vaſt boſom ſleep!
At whoſe command the foaming billows roar,
Yet know their limits, tremble, and adore.

VIII.

Let the wide world his praiſes ſing,
From whom their various bleſſings ſpring,
Let echoing anthems make his praiſes known
On earth, his footſtool, as in heaven his throne.

THE END.

ERRATA.

PAGE 4. line 20. read *sacred joy*. P. 12. l. 16. read *diviner*. P. 30. l. 3. read *stormy*. P. 37. l. 14. read *bear*. P. 54. last l. read *concert*. P. 68. Those verses of the 63d. Psalm after the first Pause, should have been printed as a separate Psalm, or entirely omitted; as they are a different Metre from the first part, and some of them were used before. P. 77. l. 14. for *their* read *the*. P. 105. for *its* read *his*. P. 107. l. 2. read, *his name is love*. P. 125. l. 7. for *breath*, read *breast*.

AN ALPHABETICAL TABLE

Of the First Lines of all the PSALMS.

A	Page
ALMIGHTY GOD thy pow'rful word	2
Almighty maker GOD	62
And now, my soul, another year	151
Arise, my soul, on wings devout arise	39
Arise and hail the happy day	155
As the good shepherd gently leads	16

B

BE thou exalted, O my GOD	63
Behold the morning sun	135
Bless thou the LORD, my soul, his name	107
Blest is the man who fears the LORD	121
Blest are the sons of peace	127

C

COME we who love the LORD	148
Come sound his praise abroad	149

E

ETERNAL GOD, almighty cause	27
Eternal source of ev'ry joy	50

F

FATHER of all! eternal mind?	153
Father of all, in ev'ry age	162
From all who dwell below the skies	76

An Alphabetical Table to the PSALMS.

G
          Page

GIVE thanks to GOD, the sov'reign LORD 95
Give thanks to GOD moſt high 96
Give to our GOD immortal praiſe 98
Give thanks to GOD, he reigns above 107
GOD of our lives, whoſe bounteous care 10
Good is the LORD, the heav'nly king 113
GOD of my mercies, and my praiſe 120
GOD is a ſpirit, juſt and wiſe 138
Great firſt of beings! mighty LORD! 1
Great GOD! to thee our grateful tongues 15
Great GOD! how infinite art thou! 29
Great GOD! the heav'ns well order'd frame 45
Great LORD of earth, and ſeas and ſkies 59
Great is the LORD, his works of might 76
Great is our GOD, his works of might 92
Great GOD! my joyful thanks to thee 108
GOD, who in various methods told 115

H

HAIL! voice divine! thus the almighty ſaid 9
Hail, King ſupreme! all wiſe and good 88
Happy is he who fears the LORD 123
Hark the glad ſound, the ſaviour comes 114
Hark, from on high a chearing voice 150
He who has GOD his guardian made 23
High in the heav'ns, eternal GOD 58
How are thy ſervants bleſt, O LORD 25
How bleſt is he who ne'er conſents 119
How bleſt are they who always keep 130
How pleas'd and bleſs'd was I! 131
How ſhall the young ſecure their hearts 132
How pleaſant! how divinely fair! 137

An Alphabetical Table to the PSALMS.

I
	Page
I Love the volume of thy word	136
I sing th' almighty pow'r of GOD	73
If GOD succeed not, all the cost	144
In all my vast concerns with thee	31
In GOD's own house pronounce his praise	62
Indulgent GOD, whose bounteous care	159
Is there ambition in my heart?	128
Jehovah reigns, he dwells in light	41
Joy to the world, the LORD is come	118

L
LET all the just to GOD with joy	3
Let all the earth their voices raise	43
Let ev'ry tongue thy goodness speak	53
Let ev'ry creature join	67
Let heathens to their idols haste	102
Let thanks to thee, all sov'reign pow'r arise	111
Long as we live we'll bless thy name	80
Look round, O man, survey this globe	89
LORD, unto thee we lift our eyes	22
LORD thou hast search'd and seen me thro'	32
LORD, thou art good, all nature shews	48
LORD, when I count thy mercies o'er	112
LORD, how secure and blest are they	126
LORD, who's the happy man who may	133
LORD of the worlds above	160

M
MY GOD, my everlasting hope	20
My GOD, my King, thy various praise	18
My GOD, the steps of pious men	139
My GOD, permit my tongue	143
My soul inspir'd with sacred love	54

Z

An Alphabetical Table to the PSALMS.

N
	Page
NAKED as from the earth we came	61

O
O All ye sons of human race	71
O all ye nations, praise the LORD	75
O azure vaults, O chrystal sky	164
O bless the LORD, our souls	55
O come, loud anthems let us sing	35
O, for an hymn of universal praise	82
O happy nation, where the LORD	21
O GOD, on thee we all depend	14
O GOD, our help in ages past	30
O GOD my saviour, and my king	124
O LORD, how excellent thy name	6
O LORD our heav'nly king	91
O LORD, thy bounty flows above	110
On thee, O GOD we still depend	60
On thee, each morning, O my GOD	158
O praise the LORD in that blest place	85
O render thanks to GOD above	109
Our shepherd is the living LORD	17
Our souls repeat his praise	56
O that the LORD would guide my ways	145

P
PRAISE ye the LORD, the universal King	66
Praise ye the LORD; our GOD to praise	77

R
REJOICE, ye righteous in the LORD	93
Rise, rise, my soul, and leave thy ground	28

S
SAY, should we search the globe around	156
Sing to the LORD with joyful voice	4

An Alphabetical Table to the PSALMS.

	Page
Sing to the LORD JEHOVAH's name	103
Sing to the LORD, ye diftant lands	116
Songs of immortal praife belong	44
Sweet is the mem'ry of thy grace	52

T

THAT man is bleft who ftands in awe	122
The LORD JEHOVAH reigns	13
The earth, and all the heav'nly frame	15
The LORD himfelf, the mighty LORD	18
The LORD the fov'reign king	41
The glories of our maker GOD	72
Thee I will blefs, my GOD and King	78
The heav'ns declare thy glory, LORD	86
The fpacious firmament on high	87
The LORD my pafture fhall prepare	152
This fpacious earth is all the LORD's	140
Thro' all the various fhifting fcene	57
Thus faith the LORD, the fpacious fields	129
Thy name, almighty LORD	74
Thy juftice, LORD, maintains it's throne	139
Thy works of glory, mighty LORD	24
'Tis by thy ftrength the mountains ftand	57
To heaven my grateful foul afcends	19
To GOD the mighty LORD	100
To heav'n I lift my waiting eyes	104
To our almighty maker GOD	117
'Twas from thy hand, my GOD, I came	11
'Twas GOD who fix'd the rolling fpheres	34

U and V

UPWARD I lift mine eyes	105
VAST are thy works, almighty LORD	90

An Alphabetical Table to the PSALMS.

W

	Page
WE bless the LORD, the just, the good	102
When I with pleasing wonder stand	12
When all thy mercies, O our GOD	46
Wherewith shall I approach the LORD	146
While some in folly's pleasures roll	126
Who shall inhabit in thy hill	142
With one consent let all the earth	5
With rev'rence let the saints appear	37
With chearful notes let all the earth	75
With all my pow'rs of heart and tongue	79
With glory clad, with strength array'd	94
With songs and honours sounding loud	141

Y

YE tribes of Adam, join	7
Ye sons of men in sacred lays	36
Ye holy souls in GOD rejoice	40
Ye that delight to serve the LORD	42
Ye boundless realms of joy	64

THE END.

www.ingramcontent.com/pod-product-compliance
Lightning Source LLC
Chambersburg PA
CBHW032058220426
43664CB00008B/1058